Lives of the Conjurers

Volume Two

by Professor Solomon

Illustrated by Steve Solomon

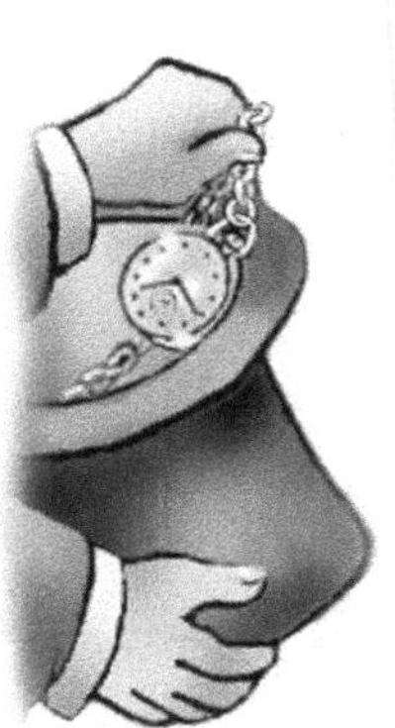

TOP HAT PRESS
BALTIMORE

ISBN 978-0-912509-16-7

http://www.professorsolomon.com

Top Hat Press
Baltimore, Maryland

Lives of the Conjurers
Volume Two

CONTENTS

Georges Méliès

GEORGES MÉLIÈS WAS BORN IN PARIS IN 1861. HIS father was a wealthy manufacturer of boots; and it was expected that Georges, along with his two older brothers, would eventually take over the business. But as a boy he revealed an artistic sensibility: constructing puppet shows; drawing caricatures of friends and teachers; filling his exercise books with doodles.

After receiving his baccalaureate (from the same lycée that Baudelaire had attended), he worked for a year in his father's factory, as an accounts supervisor. Two years in the army followed. His father then sent him to London, ostensibly to work at a dry-goods emporium and learn English. In fact, the aim was to end his romance with a woman—the daughter of a janitor—deemed unsuitable by the family.

While in London, Méliès frequented the Egyptian Hall. "England's Home of Mystery," as it was billed, was a theatre dedicated to magic. It was under the direction of John Nevil Maskelyne, the country's leading magician. Presented daily were large-scale illusions, embedded in dramatic sketches—a new and popular format. These shows fascinated Méliès.

Returning to Paris, he wanted to study painting at the École des Beaux-Arts; but his father refused to fund such an endeavor. So he went back to work at the factory, as a supervisor of machinery. The work was not congenial to someone of Méliès's temperament. Yet it did teach him mechanical skills that would prove useful in his future occupation.

Meanwhile, he was taking conjuring lessons from the proprietor of a magic shop. And it wasn't long before Méliès was performing—initially, at the homes of friends, then at the Musée Grévin, a wax museum with a small theatre that featured magicians. He also married the daughter of a family friend. Bringing with her a sizeable dowry, Eugénie had met with the family's approval.

In 1888 his father retired. The factory was given to the three sons, who were to run it jointly. But Georges had other plans. He sold his share of the business to his brothers. And later that year he purchased a theatre.

The Théâtre Robert-Houdin was a Parisian landmark. It had been founded in 1845, at an earlier location, by Jean Eugène Robert-Houdin. An innovative magician, Robert-Houdin had rejected the wizardly garb—robe and pointed cap—and garish decor of his predecessors. Instead, "the father of modern magic" wore evening dress, and performed on a set that resembled an elegant drawing-room. Located at 8 boulevard des Italiens, the theatre was an intimate space with 225 seats. Its stage had been expressly designed for the presentation of illusions, with trapdoors, trick furniture, and other hidden features.

Méliès purchased the theatre from the widow of the magician's son. It came with the original furnishings and magical apparatus, including automata that Robert-Houdin had built. The theatre was still serving as a venue for magic acts, but had become neglected and rundown. Méliès refurbished it, revitalized its offerings, and brought the place back to life.

Only occasionally, however, did he perform in his theatre. Instead, he served as producer, director, writer, and set designer. He also created new illusions, constructing the apparatus himself. Veteran magicians were hired to perform them. Like those at the Egyptian Hall, the illusions were embedded in dramatic sketches.*

The sketches had titles like *La Source enchantée* ("The Enchanted Spring"), *Le Nain jaune* ("The Yellow Dwarf"), and *L'Auberge du Diable* ("The Devil's Inn"). Typically, they

---

* During this period Méliès also founded the Académie de Prestidigitation, a fraternal organization, and served as its president. It was a union for magicians. Among its aims was to improve the reception of itinerant magicians in the towns they visited. And he was drawing political cartoons for a newspaper.

were comic pantomimes, accompanied by piano, that linked a series of illusions. During an intermission, the automata—which Méliès had restored to working order—could be viewed in the lobby. Also on display were such marvels as the Mirror of Cagliostro, in which one's reflection became a vaseful of flowers, then the face of a lovely woman. And the evening concluded with magic-lantern slides. Projected onto a screen were scenic views, fantastical vistas, and caricatures drawn by Méliès.

Altogether, Méliès would produce about thirty of these sketches. And there might have been more, had it not been for an exhibition at the Grand Café that he attended on December 28, 1895. This historic event—hosted by the Lumière brothers, proprietors of a photographic firm—marked the birth of the cinema.

Actually, animated photographs were nothing new. Edison's Kinetoscope—a peepshow machine, into which one peered to view short films—had been around since 1893. But the Lumières were the first to successfully *project* films (or at least, to do so before a paying audience). They accomplished this with their Cinématographe—a boxlike device that functioned as both a camera, for recording a series of images, and a projector, for bringing them to life on a screen. Earlier in the year the brothers had held a private demonstration of their invention. Now they were presenting it to the public—as a scientific curiosity, for they had as yet no further plans for it. Ten films, each about a minute long, were shown that day at the Grand Café.

Everyone in the audience was spellbound by the flickering images on the screen. And no one more so than Georges Méliès, who immediately saw them as an attraction for his theatre—a new kind of illusion. He approached the brothers and asked to buy a Cinématographe. But none was available, he was told.

So in March he traveled to London and bought a similar device: the Theatrograph (also known as the Animatographe). The Theatrograph was described as a "projecting Kinetoscope." It had been invented by Robert Paul, a maker of electrical instruments, who manufactured and sold Kinetoscopes. (Edison had neglected to patent the Kinetoscope outside the U.S.) The Theatrograph was essentially a magic lantern, modified to project a series of images from a strip of film.

On April 4, 1896, at the Théâtre Robert-Houdin, Méliès —using what he would call the Kinétograph—showed his first films. Billed as "*photographies animées,*" they replaced the magic-lantern slides at the end of the show. The audience marveled at the moving pictures that filled the screen. Waves rolling into shore! A boxing match between two kangaroos! Intended for Kinetoscopes, these brief films had been created by Edison and Paul.

Méliès was the first magician to embrace moving pictures. But others in the profession soon followed his lead, acquiring projectors and including films in their acts. At the nearby (and rival) Théâtre Isola, the Isola brothers showed films, projected with an Isolatographe, as they called it. Leopoldo Fregoli—a magician, mimic, and quick-change artist—showed films with a Fregoligraph. Professor Anderson (who claimed to be the son of the renowned Professor Anderson) showed them with his Andersonoscopograph. And John Nevil Maskelyne featured films at the Egyptian Hall. Modestly, he called his projector simply a Mutagraph.

Thus, magicians were among the pioneers of the cinema. They were the first customers for projectors, and the first exhibitors of films. In *Marvelous Méliès,* Paul Hammond explains:

> It is perfectly natural that a superior optical illusion like the cinema should find itself initially in the hands of conjurors, who are often expert mechanics, and are well acquainted with optical trickery, such as mirror masking, reflected images, transparent reflections, lantern projection, background work and chiaroscuro.

Audiences were enthralled by the photographies animées; and Méliès wanted to make them a regular part of the show. But the supply of films available to him was limited. So he modified the Theatrograph to serve as a camera and began to make his own. Initially, Méliès filmed in the backyard of his home in Montreuil, a suburb of Paris. Family and friends enacted such ordinary activities as playing cards and gardening. Later that summer, while vacationing in Normandy, he filmed the beach during a storm, the arrival of a train, and similar scenes.

These animated snapshots were just the beginning. Méliès had launched himself on a new career as a filmmaker. During the next fifteen years he would make more than 500 films. They varied in length from less than a minute to half-an-hour. The catalogue of Star Films, as he branded his productions, included "newsreels" (re-creations of major events, such as *The Coronation of Edward VII*) and historical dramas. But most of his films were trick films—a genre in which Méliès was the master. They featured illusions inspired by those in his stage shows. For he had discovered the magical possibilities of the cinema. By stopping and starting the camera, or by double-exposing the film, Méliès found that he could create startling illusions.

The Vanishing Lady, for example, is a film adaptation of one of his stage acts—one that adds a new twist to the original. The set resembles the stage of the Théâtre Robert-Houdin. Méliès himself, costumed as a magician, brings out the lady, who is played by Jehanne d'Alcy, his lead actress and his mistress. He seats her in a chair and covers her with a drape. When the drape is removed, the lady has disappeared. In the stage version, she then emerged from the wings. Here, Méliès waves magically—and to his dismay, a skeleton appears, seated in the chair! Go away, he gestures, and covers the skeleton with the drape. When the drape is removed, the lady is back in the chair. It was camera magic as effective as anything on the stage. And no trapdoor was required.*

* *The Vanishing Lady* may currently be viewed on YouTube. Go to http://youtu.be/f7-x93QagJU, or search for "Vanishing Lady Melies."

These trick films were filmed as tableaux, in long shot. Melies wanted them to resemble a stage performance. The stories were both fantastical and farcical. Typical is that of Méliès's most famous film, *A Trip to the Moon* (1902). A group of astronomers board a spaceship; and a giant cannon propels it toward the moon. There the astronomers are captured by moon men—weird, cavorting creatures (played by acrobats from the Folies-Bergère), who, when struck, explode and disappear. They escape from the moon men, return to earth, and are acclaimed as heroes.*

The films of Méliès are rarely without magical effects. A figure comes alive and steps out of a portrait. Devils materialize out of nowhere, create mischief, and vanish. A musician (played by Méliès) replicates himself into six additional musicians—each with a different instrument; and they perform as an ensemble. A head on a table is inflated, to its dismay, with a bellows; expands like a balloon; and explodes. (The head is Méliès's.) And fanciful, extravagant sets lend a magical quality to the films.

The sets were designed by Méliès himself. Like that replicating musician, he was an *homme-orchestre*—a one-man band—of the cinema. He produced, wrote, and directed

* *A Trip to the Moon* may currently be viewed on YouTube. Go to https://www.youtube.com/watch?v=_FrdVdKlxUk, or search for "Trip to the Moon Melies."

the films. He designed the costumes and supervised the camera. And he was often the lead actor. His favorite role was that of Mephistopheles, whom he portrayed with gusto in a number of films.

So popular were the photographies animées at his theatre that Méliès made them the entire show. Beginning in the fall of 1897, the evening shows consisted entirely of films; only at matinees was stage magic still performed. The Théâtre Robert-Houdin had become a movie theatre. And Méliès now devoted all of his energies to filmmaking. Behind his home in Montreuil he had built a studio. It had glass walls to admit sunlight (electric arc-lights would eventually be installed); stage machinery; and a cabin for the camera. The stage was the exact size of the stage at the theatre. As he prospered, additional facilities were built: a film lab, a carpentry shop, a costume storage. Behind the house in which he resided with his family arose a full-fledged movie studio. It even had a commissary, where a midday meal, hosted by Méliès, was shared by the entire crew.

Originally, his films were shown only at the Théâtre Robert-Houdin. But there was a market for them elsewhere; and Méliès sought it out. His first customers were at fairgrounds, where animated photographs became a sideshow attraction. And he was soon selling prints to theatres in France, England, and the U.S. To secure an American copyright for the films and thus prevent bootlegging, Méliès opened an office in New York. It was manned by his brother Gaston, who had gone to work for Star Films.*

Star Films continued for years as a successful enterprise. But the cinema was evolving; and eventually Méliès got left behind. His style of filmmaking—farces with magical effects, staged as tableaux—never changed. But such films had fallen out of favor with audiences. Moreover, the pro-

* Gaston would become a filmmaker himself. He produced more than one hundred short Westerns, shot on location in Texas and California. As with silent films in general, few of these have survived.

duction of films had become increasingly industrialized; and independent artists like Méliès were an anachronism. Once an innovative pioneer, he had become a relic. *The Voyage of the Family Bourrichon*, made in 1912, would prove to be his final film. He had borrowed money to make it; and when it failed commercially (as had his last few films), Méliès found himself broke and in debt.

The years that followed were bleak. In 1913 his wife Eugénie died. And during the war the Army requisitioned the offices of Star Films in Paris; confiscated hundreds of films; and melted them down. The chemicals were used for the manufacture of heels for military boots.

After the war he was forced to sell the property at Montreuil—his home, his studio, and a variety theatre that he had been operating with his son and daughter—in order to pay his debts. Scenery, props, and costumes were sold, as well as the remaining prints of his films. In a moment of anger, Méliès burnt his store of negatives. And in 1923 the Théâtre Robert-Houdin—taken from him for a paltry sum—was torn down, to clear the way for an extension of the boulevard Haussmann. The last link with his former life—with those years as a magician and filmmaker—was gone. Or so it seemed.

But then Jehanne d'Alcy, the actress who had played the Vanishing Lady, reappeared in his life. Years before, she had been his mistress and leading lady. But her fortunes, too, had declined. She was now a widow, who was selling toys and candy at a kiosk in the Montparnasse train station. They resumed their friendship, married, and ran the kiosk together. The station was cold in the winter, sweltering in the summer. Amid the flow of travelers, Méliès—Mephistopheles!—sold pop-guns, yo-yos, dolls. No one gave him a second look. He and his films had been forgotten by the public.

Méliès would refer to this period of his life as "a true martyrdom." But the Wheel of Fortune keeps turning. Those whom it has brought low may yet be raised again. And in the late 1920s Georges Méliès and his films were rediscovered. Some cinema enthusiasts had learned, to their surprise, that he was still alive. (One of them had been walking past the kiosk; and overhearing the proprietor addressed as "monsieur Méliès," had stopped to speak with him.) And a small cache of his films had been found. The result was the organizing of a retrospective. A Gala Méliès was held, with the guest of honor bursting through a paper screen to make his entrance. Those found films—among them *A Trip to the Moon*—were shown, to fervid applause.*

A petition was circulated by notables in the film industry, calling for an official honor. As a result, the French government bestowed upon Méliès the Legion of Honor. In *Artificially Arranged Scenes: The Films of Georges Méliès*, John Frazer describes his final years:

> In 1931 at a grand banquet, Méliès was at last recognized for his pioneering achievement and was awarded the Legion of Honor by Louis Lumière, who saluted Méliès as the "creator of cinematographic spectacles." At long last, in 1932, Méliès was able to leave the drafty cold of the Gare Montparnasse. A mutual organization for people of the motion pictures had been founded and that organization had acquired an estate near Orly Airport. Méliès, his wife, and granddaughter were given a three-room apartment which Méliès occupied until his death. There he spent his time drawing, telling stories of the early days of magic and movies, and answering the inquiries of film historians.

---

* Copies of his films would continue to be found, in barns, attics, and other unlikely places. A major trove turned up in the possession of the widow of Leon Schlesinger, producer of the "Merry Melodies" and "Looney Tunes" cartoons. When Star Films collapsed, Gaston Méliès had sold these prints and negatives to Vitagraph—a company that later merged with Warner Brothers. Recognizing the films as a treasure, Schlesinger had bought them from Warner Brothers.

About 200 of Méliès's films have thus far been found.

Charlier

AMONG PERFORMERS OF CARD TRICKS, A STANDARD flourish is the Charlier Cut: the cutting of a deck of cards with one hand. The technique was originated by a legendary figure—a magician whom Henry Ridgely Evans calls "the arch-master of card-conjuring." Little is known about Charlier. In *The Old and the New Magic* (1909), Evans describes the aura of mystery that surrounded him:

> Some say that Charlier taught card manipulation to Robert-Houdin in Paris, and instructed many other famous professionals of the Continent. Some say he was a German, some a Frenchman, some a Turk, some a Russian, some an Italian, some a Greek. Some men say he was the "Wandering Jew," Ahasuerus, about whom so many legends cluster. No one seems to know exactly who he was. He spoke many languages well, and preserved the secret of his identity and nationality. He appeared mysteriously in London, and as mysteriously disappeared. I ask again who was this sphinx-like Charlier, this one man, possessed of such astonishing vitality; dried up like a mummy, yet vigorous as a fellow of twenty? Conjurers regarded him with awe.

The magician who knew him best during his stay in London was Charles Bertram, a court favorite with the title of "Conjurer to His Royal Highness the Prince of Wales." In his memoirs Bertram provides a vivid description of Charlier:

> He came to my house one day about fourteen years ago, and introduced himself to me, saying that he had heard that I took some interest in conjuring, and that he would like to make my acquaintance. He was an old man. From

> his appearance he might have been anything between seventy and ninety. He had a thin, clean-shaven face, of parchment-like appearance, full of wrinkles; thin; long hair, gray and unkempt; a mouth firmly closed; long, thin, Jewish type of nose; and small piercing eyes. He wore an old tall silk hat, black and rather seedy-looking clothes.... He had been a tall man, I should say, perhaps six feet in height, but his shoulders were slightly bent with age. He walked with a very firm step, and very quickly, always carrying with him a small black bag. He spoke nine or ten languages fluently, including English, was very distinct in his pronunciation, biting off his words, as it were, sharply and crisply. His manner was exceedingly polite and gentlemanly, and if he was quick to rebuke a familiarity, was equally quick to pardon or accept an apology, very aristocratic in his bearing, but having at times somewhat of the style of an autocrat. (*Isn't It Wonderful?*, 1896)

Once they had become acquainted, the two men met frequently. Charlier would teach card tricks to Bertram. He also tutored him in the methods of "grecs," or card sharpers. Though impoverished, Charlier would accept no payment for these lessons. When Bertram did offer to pay, Charlier "would look disdainfully at me, and would leave me without a word." On each visit, he brought a gift for Bertram's wife. He would hand it to her "with a long, earnest speech, generally attributing to these little gifts some potent or mysterious property, and so impressing these facts upon her that oftentimes she was quite frightened even to look at or handle them."

To support himself, Charlier went about as a busker. He roamed from pub to pub, in Covent Garden, St. Martin's Lane, and the Strand, doing card tricks and passing the hat. He also gave private lessons. ("What he could do with a pack of cards cannot be described in words," one of his students would recall. "It had to be seen to be believed. He was a marvel in all that related to card manipulation.") And he was a craftsman. For magicians and others, Charlier prepared decks of marked cards. Painstakingly, he pricked each card with a fine-pointed needle. These pin-pricks were

detectable by touch; and their location revealed the identity of the card. The method became known as the Charlier System.

Angelo Lewis (who, as "Professor Hoffmann," wrote *Magic*, *More Magic*, and *Later Magic*, the classic texts on conjuring) deemed Charlier to be "the greatest of living card experts." Lewis once paid a visit to his lodgings:

> His chronic condition was one of poverty. I called upon him once, and once only, and found him in bed, in a side-street off the Strand, occupying a room about twelve feet by eight, which appeared to be his sitting-room, bedroom, and workshop. His work was preparing cards (beveled, punctured, etc.), which he did with marvelous dexterity.

Rumors abounded as to his origins. He was said to be an Alsatian. (Although fluent in English, Charlier often lapsed into French.) Or the illegitimate son of a Grand Duke, who had left Russia after getting into trouble over card-playing.

Or the illegitimate son of the Duke of Hamilton and a Polish woman. John Nevil Maskelyne (who bought a deck of marked cards from him) was convinced that Charlier had been a card sharper:

> I think he must have been a card sharper in his younger days, for he used many of the sleights of the gambler.... He had exceedingly long fingers. I never saw anyone work the single-handed pass as he did, and he kept the skin at the end of his right thumb so sensitive that he could detect a projection [from a pin-prick] upon the back of a card, quite invisible to sight and imperceptible to ordinary touch.

Charlier remained in London for five years. But in June 1884 he informed a student that their next session would be the last. And he told Angelo Lewis that he was preparing to visit Boulogne, where he had friends. Bertram recounts what followed:

> One day an old friend of mine and a great friend of Charlier's, came to me and told me that Charlier's landlady had not been able to get into his room, and that as he (Charlier) had not been seen for some days, had fetched assistance and had his door broken open, when Charlier was found lying on his bed, dead. I told him I could scarcely believe it, and that I felt sure he would have sent for me had he been in trouble or want. He replied that it was perfectly true, that the little furniture and his clothes had been sold, and that he had been buried. About three months after this when calling upon my old friend Doncaster...he said to me, "Did you not tell me that Charlier was dead?" "Certainly," I replied. "No," he said, "he is not. He came in here yesterday afternoon, and said he was going to Naples to be married." That is the last I have heard of Charlier. I have never set eyes upon him since, and I am still in doubt whether he died or married—a remarkable exit for a truly mysterious man.

Twenty years later, Henry Ridgely Evans set out to write about Charlier. A diligent researcher, Evans spoke or corresponded with persons who had known him; pored over books and records; and contacted Trewey, a veteran entertainer in France. Trewey recalled a magician named Arelier, who had performed in Nice back in 1874. The description of Arelier matched that of Charlier.

And a correspondent in San Francisco described a magician who called himself Carabaraba, and who had performed there in 1876. His physical appearance was similar to that of Charlier. Fluent in many languages, Carabaraba had told the correspondent that he was originally from Jerusalem. And although ninety years old, he had displayed the agility of a much younger man. "He was the most skilful manipulator of cards I ever saw. He told me he had been all over the world, and had performed in all the principal cities of the Orient and Occident. He was a mystery to all of us in San Francisco. We called him the 'Wandering Jew.'"

In *The Old and the New Magic* Evans tells what is known about Charlier. "Farewell Prince of Pasteboards [playing cards]," he concludes, "doubtless by this time you have shuffled your last pack of cards in shuffling off this mortal coil." For Evans assumed that Charlier was no longer among the living.

But after the book was published, he received a letter. It had been mailed from Atlantic City. And it was from Charlier! (Or at least, it bore his signature.) Charlier complimented Evans on the book, but offered some corrections to the account of his stay in London.

Was the letter authentic? Years later, Evans was still wondering. In an article titled "Magicians Who Have Disappeared," he reveals his doubts:

> I did not reply to the letter, fearing to be the victim of a hoax. But did the missive, which was couched in such polite terms, emanate from the real Charlier? Twenty-seven years have passed since the above mentioned incident. I shall never know the truth now, I feel assured. Perhaps when I have gone hence, I shall meet... the clever manipulator of "pasteboards" in the Elysian Fields and find out all about him.

De Sarak

On the evening of March 15, 1902, in Washington, D.C., Dr. Albert de Sarak gave a demonstration of his psychic powers. Several hundred persons had crowded into a hall to see him. Among them was a reporter from the *Washington Post.*

The next day the newspaper published an account of the event. De Sarak—described by the *Post* as "occultist and adept, a professor of the mystical and the sixth sense"—had come onto the stage with a young woman. One of his followers, she would be serving as an interpreter. For while de Sarak claimed to speak fourteen languages, he was not fluent in English.

The interpreter introduced him. De Sarak was the descendant of a noble French family, she said. Yet he had been born in Tibet, and had been educated in schools there and among adepts hidden in the mountains. He had devoted his life to the study of the occult. And he was now touring the world and sharing his knowledge with mankind.

Then de Sarak began to speak—in French—as the young woman translated. He was wearing a white turban and a yellow robe. Mystical emblems hung from a chain around his neck. With his pointed black beard and otherworldly gaze, he seemed the very model of a mystic from Tibet.

De Sarak described his powers. They were related to second sight, he said, and utilized a "wonderful fluid force"—an energy that was latent in all men. This same force had been known to the ancient Egyptians, who had used it to levitate the stones for the pyramids. His powers were not supernatural, he emphasized; they merely caused a "hastening of nature's work."

And for the rest of the evening, he performed feats that were made possible by that force—feats that amazed his audience.

The first of these was a transformation of fish eggs. The *Post* described it:

> A glass plate, with a number of fish eggs, was shown and examined. A large glass bowl was filled with water, and one of the members of the audience was told to carefully brush the eggs into the water. In the meantime three men from the audience had with strong ropes securely bound the hands of the adept behind his back as he sat in the chair. Broad, clean, white cloths were wrapped about the seated figure, leaving the head free, and the three men selected held the cloths in place. Music rolled from a deep organ, and the head of the adept sank back and a strange light appeared to cross his face. According to the directions of the interpreter the bowl of water containing the fish eggs was placed by one of the three beneath the cloths on the lap of the adept.
>
> After a period of straining and soft moaning from the white-wrapped figure, for perhaps ten minutes, the cloths were removed, and from the lap of the apparently insensible man was lifted the bowl of water, but instead of the eggs which it contained a few moments before there swam about a dozen of tiny, new-born fish.

For his next feat, de Sarak was blindfolded. Wads of cotton and half-a-dozen bandages were placed over his eyes. The music swelled; and he entered into a trance. Then he descended from the stage and confidently strolled about the hall. Though unable to see, he was able to avoid obstacles and navigate the narrow aisles.

He returned to the stage and, still blindfolded, approached a blank canvas on an easel. Beside it was a set of paints. Sightlessly, he mixed colors and painted a picture.

And still blindfolded, he played a game of dominoes with a member of the audience. Earlier, de Sarak had written on a card. When the game ended, the card—which had been kept secure—was read. He was found to have correctly predicted the numbers on the final dominoes.

The evening concluded with equally astonishing feats. "Experiments were given at the close in the disintegration and restoration of matter, of psychic perception, in which he aroused the wondering admiration of the audience," reported the *Post.*

•

Three months later, a circular went out to prominent people in Washington. It was sent by the Oriental Esoteric Center, and addressed itself to "those who truly wish to understand!" Such persons were urged "to unite themselves with us in a truly fraternal chain...woven of flowers of the soul." Announced was the founding in Washington of an Order—a "movement of true progress"—whose purpose was to perpetuate the work of Dr. Albert de Sarak. De Sarak represented the Supreme Council of the Adepts, located in Tibet. He possessed powers unknown to the West, and would be using those powers, not to enrich himself, but to engage the attention of persons of high ideals. That they might "go forward, ever forward, and ever higher!"

The Order would be publishing a review. Called *The Radiant Truth,* it would contain "all that the most eager student of Occult Truth can desire." Only members of the Order would have access to this material, or to "Esoteric demonstrations of a more advanced degree." In addition, selected members would be sent to the Orient. There they would receive instruction from those entrusted with the spiritual welfare of mankind.

Persons wishing to join the Order were invited to send in an application. An address on Corcoran street was given.

"May Peace be with all Beings!"

The circular was signed by the General Secretary and seven Esoteric Members of the Order.

•

Henry Ridgely Evans had read the *Post* article, and the circular, with indignation. The author of *Magic and Its Professors* (due to be published later that year), and a professor of magic himself (albeit an amateur), Evans had recognized de Sarak for what he was—a conjurer. The eggs-into-fish trick had been around for years. "Securely-bound" hands were liberated with ease. And as for that blindfold—really now! It was not the conjurer whom it blinded; rather, the audience, duped into believing he was unable to see.

Evans could scarcely believe that de Sarak was being taken seriously; that his illusions had elicited "wondering admiration"; and that he had succeeded in passing himself off as a Tibetan adept. Clearly, the man was a charlatan. And Evans saw it as his civic duty to expose de Sarak as such. Accordingly, he contacted his friend J. Elfreth Watkins, Jr., a journalist. And together they set out to investigate Dr. Albert de Sarak.

The plan was simple. First, Watkins would interview him, supposedly for a magazine article on occultism. Then both of them would attend a meeting of the Order; see for themselves what exactly was going on; and publish their findings.

Watkins (in "A Gentleman of Thibet," co-written with Evans and published in August 1904) describes the interview:

> I addressed a letter to Dr. Sarak by post requesting an appointment. I received a prompt response in the form of a courteous note, headed "Oriental Esoteric Center of Washington," and which commenced: "Your letter, which I have received, reveals to me a man of noble sentiments." An hour was named and the letter bore the signature, "Dr. A. Count de Sarak," beneath which were inscribed several Oriental characters.
>
> I found Monsieur le Comte's house in Corcoran street, late in the appointed afternoon. It was a two-story cottage of yellow brick with English basement, and surmounting the door was an oval medallion repeating the inscription of Monsieur's letterhead. A young woman with blonde hair and blue eyes responded to my ring. I was invited upstairs, she following. Before me was the mind picture of a Lama with yellowed and wrinkled visage, vested in folds of dingy

> red, with iron pencase at his side and counting the beads of a wooden rosary; a Yoge of the great hills; who should say to me, "Just is the wheel," or "Thou hast acquired merit."
>
> I was directed to the door of the rear parlor on the main floor, and as I opened it there sat before me, at a modern roller-top desk, a man of slender build and medium height, but with one of the most striking physiognomies I have ever beheld.

His face, reports Watkins, was that of a sheik of the desert. The nose was strongly aquiline; the hair and beard, jet-black; the eyes, "huge, languid and dreamy." He wore a black frock-coat of the latest style.

De Sarak shook hands and pointed to a chair. Watkins sat down. The young woman, who would be translating, sat down beside the adept.

"Through my power of second sight," said de Sarak (in French), "was revealed to me your mission before you arrived. And now that you come, a good spirit seems to attend you, and I know that you come as a friend."

Watkins asked if he would be willing to demonstrate, for a journalist, his psychic powers. De Sarak declined to do so. But he offered to make Watkins an honorary member of the Order. This would allow him to attend one of the weekly meetings as a spectator. "All that we will require of Monsieur," said de Sarak, "is that he endeavor to learn, and to describe what he sees with absolute truth."

Noticing on the wall a picture of the Buddha, Watkins asked de Sarak if he was a Buddhist. The adept replied that he was, as were his masters in Tibet. But he had come to America to teach the science of the soul, which did not conflict with any religion.

What was his opinion of Madame Blavatsky? asked Watkins. De Sarak deemed the founder of Theosophy to have been a good person. But he described his persecution by her followers, who had waged against him "a relentless campaign of calumny." Watkins (who intended to expose him as a fraud) sought to console de Sarak, and remarked that all great causes had grown out of persecution.

Suddenly de Sarak grimaced, as if in pain. He half-closed his eyes, and stared at an object on the window sill: a piece of colored glass, mounted on a metal support. For several minutes he stared at this object, as if in a trance. He was receiving a message from his masters, whispered the interpreter. Finally, de Sarak sighed and wrote on a sheet of paper.

He then showed Watkins some scrapbooks, and translations of clippings from newspapers and journals. One of these, from an 1885 issue of *Le Figaro,* described an unusual demonstration of hypnosis. Before a committee of scientists, Dr. de Sarak (whom the article also referred to as the Comte de Das) had hypnotized a cageful of lions. Another, from *La Révue des Sciences Psychiques,* reported on an act of levitation. Before a packed house at the Sorbonne, de Sarak had entered a trance and risen two meters into the air.*

---

* Evans and Watkins appended to their account a translation of the *Le Figaro* article:

"The press was invited yesterday by a committee of scientists to the Folies Bergères at 2 p.m. to be present at some most extraordinary and altogether novel experiments in magnetism and fascination. A subject asleep under the influence of the suggestion of the Thibetan Occultist Comte de Das, penetrated with him into a cage where were seven lions.

"Doctor de Sarak, the magnetizer, succeeded in producing in his subject, the beautiful and intelligent Mlle. Lucie X * * * all the hypnotic states, from ecstasy with the most unstable attitudes, to most terrible catalepsy with contraction of all the muscles and deathlike rigidity.

"Then she was placed by the Comte de Das horizontally, feet and head resting on two stools, and the lions lashed by the trainer Giacometti, passed backwards and forwards on this human bridge with uneasy roars and with prodigious bounds.

"Then, all at once, Dr. de Sarak, making use of that Occult Force of which he spoke to us in his lecture at the Salle des Capucines, threw the seven lions into a state of fascination, so profound that they fell to the ground like corpses, led Mlle. Lucie out of the cage and awakened her amid the applause of all the distinguished guests who had assembled to witness the experiment.

"We congratulate the learned Occultist on the well-deserved

The interview ended as Watkins had hoped:

> It was agreed that my name should be presented to the council as suggested, and two days later I received a letter notifying me of my election as honorary member of the center, congratulating me thereupon and inviting me to be present at the next meeting. I was given the privilege of bringing a friend with me. I informed Mr. Evans, and we agreed to attend the next séance, and make careful mental notes of the events of the evening.

•

Henry Ridgely Evans describes their arrival at the meeting:

> Mr. Watkins and I went together on the appointed evening to the house of the Mage, located in quaint little Corcoran street. It was a stormy night, late in November; just the sort of evening for a gathering of modern witches and wizards, in an up-to-date *Walpurgis Nacht.* We were admitted by the interpreter and secretary, whom I afterwards learned was Miss Agnes E. Marsland, graduate of the University of Cambridge, England.
>
> In the back parlor upstairs we were greeted by the Doctor, who wore a sort of Masonic collar of gold braid, upon which was embroidered a triangle. He presented us to his wife and child, who were conspicuously foreign in appearance, the latter about five years old. We were then introduced to an elderly woman, stout and with gray hair, who, we were told, was the president of the center. She wore a cordon similar to Dr. Sarak's, and soon after our arrival she rapped with a small gavel upon a table, located in the bay window of the front drawing-room.

---

triumph he has gained at the risk of his life, and we look forward to his approaching Conference at the Salle de la Sorbonne, when we shall speak again of this indefatigable propagandist of Occult Science, who is the one topic of conversation in our Scientific World today."

Seated at the table were de Sarak and the interpreter, along with the president and five other women. No one else was in attendance, save for the adept's wife and child, seated on a sofa, and three guests: Evans, Watkins, and another journalist. The three were relegated to chairs along the wall. An air of mystery pervaded the room. The walls were draped with Oriental rugs. A yellow cloth, embroidered with occult symbols, covered the table. On the table were a candelabrum, an incense burner, and a book that de Sarak was perusing. Candles and incense had been lit. At the front of the room, noted Evans, was a statue of the Buddha, "who smiled placidly and benignly at the strange gathering."

De Sarak began by expressing disappointment, that only six members—out of forty-two—had shown up that evening. He went on to deliver a lengthy discourse. Speaking in French, he talked about psychic research, and about Tibet. "The women watched their hierophant with intense fascination," reports Watkins, "save the interpreter, who maintained her saintly gaze up into space, and the wife, who sat by in sublime nonchalance."

Upon completing his talk, de Sarak left the room. He returned wearing a blue robe. In his hand was that piece of colored glass, via which he had communicated with his masters in Tibet. Placing it on the table, he made passes over it with his fingers. He was sensitizing it, he explained, with a secret fluid.

"I demonstrated at the last meeting," said de Sarak, "how this power—which I called 'yud'—could be exerted against human beings. You remember that I caused the man to fall from his bicycle. Tonight I will exert the power against an animal."

He described what he was about to do. The lights would be extinguished; and everyone was to go to the front windows and watch the street. When a horse happened to come by, he was going to send out a mental command. And the horse would come to a halt and remain motionless! De Sarak turned to Watkins. In which direction, eastward or westward, would he prefer the horse to be passing? Eastward, said Watkins.

The lights were extinguished. The six members and the guests stationed themselves by the windows. De Sarak asked that silence be maintained. Outside, a single lamp illuminated the street.

They watched in anticipation, as twenty minutes went by. Then hoofbeats were heard. And a buggy, drawn by a single horse, came down the street—traveling westward. It kept on going and disappeared from view.

Minutes later, hoofbeats were again heard; and a buggy, similar in appearance to the first, came from the opposite direction. As it neared the house, de Sarak sent out his mental command. And the horse slowed its pace, coming to a halt directly in front of the house.

The driver was heard to say: "What's the matter with that horse? Never seen him act that way before." Shaking the reins and calling out, he got the horse to resume its progress along the street.

Abuzz with astonishment, the members returned to their seats.

De Sarak gave two more demonstrations of his powers. Blindfolded, he painted a picture of a house. It was the house in Tibet, he said, where he had been initiated into the mysteries. And he elicited gasps with the disappearance

of a cigarette.

A bag was passed for donations. The president then pounded her gavel, and the meeting was adjourned.

•

Evans was an amateur magician. He had this to say about the psychic powers of Dr. Albert de Sarak:

> Is it not strange that people can take such performances seriously? The cigarette test—an old one—and familiar to every schoolboy who dabbles in legerdemain, was a mere trick, dependent upon clever substitution and palming. The absurd splatterdash which the Mage painted while blindfolded had nothing of Thibetan architecture about it, but resembled a ruined castle on the Rhine. That he was able to peep beneath his bandages at one stage of the proceedings seems to me evident.... The horse episode was of course a pre-arranged affair, yet I admit it was very well worked up and gave one a creepy feeling—thanks to the mise en scène.

The wonder-worker from Tibet was clearly a conjurer!

Some months later, de Sarak was reported to be organizing a tour. He had invited members of the Order—and anyone else who was interested—to accompany him on a journey to sacred sites in the Orient.

But the only person to set out on this journey, says Evans, was de Sarak himself, "and he, I understand, got no farther than New York City, where the French *table de hôte* abounds, and magic and mystery are chiefly to be studied in the recipes of French *chefs de cuisine.*" De Sarak had bid farewell to Washington in January 1904, leaving the Oriental Esoteric Center in the hands of Agnes Marsland, his secretary and interpreter. A paucity of donations may have induced him to move on.

Who was this conjurer, who had posed as a Tibetan adept? According to the president of the Institut Métapsychique International—who had known de Sarak at the end of his career and described him as "*ce charlatan audacieux, cynique et vaniteux*"—he was an Italian named Alberto Sartini-Sgaluppi. But he had operated under a succession of names and titles: le Commandeur Sartini Chevalier d'Albert, le Chevalier Sartini de Rosarno, le Comte de Das, le Magnétiseur Sartini, le Comte Alberto de Sarak, and finally, le Docteur Comte Albert de Sarak—that "magnetizer" who had hypnotized lions before a committee of scientists, and levitated at the Sorbonne.

Max Malini

THE BOWERY (ORIGINALLY AN INDIAN FOOTPATH, THEN the road to the outlying farms, or *bouwerijen*, of the Dutch) was once Manhattan's most fashionable street. Arrayed along it, during the early years of the republic, were mansions, fine shops, banks, and theatres. The well-to-do resided, shopped, and attended plays on the Bowery.

But by 1888—the year Max Katz, age fifteen, became a waiter at a Bowery saloon—its character had radically changed. The theatre district had moved further uptown, as had the shops; the mansions had been replaced by tenements; and an elevated train now rumbled over a concourse of thriving but less-than-genteel entertainments. ("The livest mile on the face of the globe," it was called.) Among the entertainments were dime museums; and the most popular of these was the Globe. Visitors to the Globe could roam about and explore its miscellany of attractions. They could peer at the curiosities (often fake) in display cases; at the waxwork figures; at Chang the Chinese Giant and other human exhibits. They could listen to the mechanical music of the Orchestrion. And they could file into the Globe's theatre to watch a puppet show or a magic act.

Arrayed along the Bowery now were dime museums, dance halls, pool halls, concert halls (with food, drink, and bawdy shows), faro halls (faro was a popular card game), vaudeville houses, shooting galleries, and German beer gardens. For sailors there were tattoo parlors; for newcomers to the city, lodging houses; for the jobless, employment agencies and pawn shops. Brothels operated with impunity. There was not a single church—only the Bowery Mission (still in operation today).

And there were saloons—nearly a hundred of them—with nickel beers and rowdy companionship. The best known was Steve Brodie's at 114 Bowery. Brodie was famous for having jumped off the Brooklyn Bridge, on a bet, and survived (though he may have faked the jump with a dummy). On display at his saloon were a painting of the stunt and an affidavit from the barge captain who had pulled him from the water. Gombossy's, at 294 Bowery, was a hangout for crooks. Paddy Martin's, at 9 Bowery, had an opium den in the basement. And Seiden's had singing waiters—one of whom was Max Katz.

Seiden's was run by Professor Seiden, a magician who had won the saloon in a poker game. Seiden (who was also a ventriloquist and fire-eater) billed himself as "the modern Mephistopheles." His catch-phrase was "Watch the Professor!" And no one watched him more closely than young Katz. For "Ketzele," as his employer called him, had become Seiden's pupil. When not serving beers, he was learning sleight of hand, misdirection, and other skills from his mentor. He would practice them on the patrons in the saloon.

For an aspiring magician it was the best education imaginable—an apprenticeship with a veteran performer. During his time at Seiden's saloon, Katz developed both his conjuring skills and his self-confidence. With a captive (and inebriated) audience, he perfected routines; learned how to handle himself; and developed a style. Eventually, he began to perform elsewhere on the Bowery. Going from saloon to saloon, he would entertain with tricks and pass the hat—a barroom busker.

It is unclear how long he continued to perform in saloons. But by the turn of the century, Katz had moved on to more profitable venues. He had developed an impressive, full-length act. And he had adopted a stage name: Max Malini.

Although one of the most successful magicians of his time, Malini was an anomaly. For he was not well-known to the general public. Nor did he perform in theatres or have an agent. Rather, he was an itinerant magician—a throwback to an earlier era—"the last of the mountebanks," as he has been called. Traveling about (and during his fifty-year career, he traveled more than any other magician), he put on shows in banquet rooms, private clubs, and homes. He traveled light, with no paraphernalia, stage set, or posters. Nor did Malini have an assistant. For his unique brand of magic he needed only nimble fingers, a tableful of ordinary items, and a masterful stage presence.

The banquet rooms were located in hotels. Arriving in a city, he would check into a hotel and reserve the ballroom or other function room. He would then hang out in the hotel's bar—and in other bars—and drum up business. Malini would introduce himself to the bar's patrons as a magician, and entertain them with impromptu magic—simple but mystifying tricks with beer glasses, coins, cigarettes, cards, or whatever was handy. Such were his sleight-of-hand abilities, and the force of his personality, that Malini charmed his newfound friends. He then informed them that he'd be giving a show at the hotel, and that tickets were available. He urged them to attend, and also to spread the word. Word-of-mouth is an effective means of advertising; and the shows were well-attended.*

Malini did well financially with these hotel events. But he had an even more lucrative source of income. For he had become a "society entertainer"—a magician who was hired by the well-to-do to come to their homes and entertain their guests. Engagements of this sort became his specialty. They had begun as the result of a publicity coup that Malini scored in January 1902, in Washington. He was visiting the Capitol building, when he spotted Mark Hanna, the powerful senator from Ohio. Approaching Hanna, he introduced himself as a magician; leaned forward; and, with a ripping sound, *bit off a button from Hanna's jacket.* (Or so it seemed.) The senator was dumbfounded. Malini stood there

* A true itinerant, Malini had no permanent home for most of his adult life; instead, he stayed at hotels. He became well-known in the bars of those hotels; and long after his death, bartenders told stories of the impromptu magic he had performed there.

During his frequent visits to New York, he always stayed at the Waldorf-Astoria. On display in its bar was a paving stone, inscribed "This stone was magically produced by Max Malini."

with the button between his teeth, a thread dangling from it. Then, placing the button back onto the jacket, he magically restored it.*

The story of his biting off and restoring Mark Hanna's button was reported in local newspapers, and taken up by the wire services. Mystified and amused, Hanna invited Malini to his home, to entertain a gathering of friends. He

---

* This trick is illustrative of Malini's methods. He carried with him an assortment of jacket buttons, each with a thread dangling from it. Before approaching Hanna, he selected a button that resembled those on the senator's jacket and palmed it. Then he accosted Hanna and seemingly bit off one of his buttons. In actuality, he had covered that button with his thumb, concealing it from view; substituted the palmed button; and pretended to bite it off. Restoring Hanna's button was thus a simple matter—for it had never left the jacket. Today, a bodyguard would have wrestled Malini to the ground before he had completed the trick.

also arranged for him to perform in the Marble Room of the Capitol building, before a group of congressmen. In both places Malini was a hit; and his career as a society entertainer was launched.

Suddenly in demand at fashionable parties, Max Malini became a sensation. He was "startling all Washington with his tricks" (New York *Herald*); "has set all Washington by the ear" (*Baltimore-American*); "is the talk of the capital" (Pittsburgh *Leader*). "Malini entered Washington as an obscure card manipulator. He leaves it famous, in the short space of three months" (Troy *Daily Times*).

With his newfound celebrity, he was even able to visit the White House. Henry Ridgely Evans, in the March 1903 issue of *The Sphinx* (a magic journal), tells of the visit:

> Malini, a genuine wizard with the pasteboards [playing cards], obtained a three-minute interview with President Roosevelt, in order to show him a few tricks with cards. Arrangements for the interview were made by a journalistic friend of Malini, who knew the President. "I am awfully busy, Mr. Malini," said the good-natured Roosevelt, "and can only accord you three minutes." But the clever little Malini spun out the time to half-an-hour, so interested did the President become.

"A remarkable young man and a remarkable performance," said Roosevelt (who, from his days as a police commissioner in New York, remembered Malini as a busker in saloons).

Malini spent that summer in Newport, entertaining at the palatial homes of the wealthy. But his ambitions were not yet satisfied. And he was soon packing a bag, boarding a ship, and crossing the Atlantic. He bore letters of introduction—from two senators—to the American ambassador in London.

The ambassador introduced him to the upper levels of British society. And in a single week Malini performed before the Lord Mayor of London, the Prime Minister, and the Prince and Princess of Wales. More engagements followed. "Malini, the American card conjurer, is the rage of

London just now," wrote the correspondent for a New York newspaper, "and no smart affair is complete unless he is engaged to mystify the guests with his amazing tricks, performed with his audience crowded around him."

Even the Queen watched him perform. The London *Chronicle* reported:

> The entertainer known as Malini recently performed some of his card tricks before a gathering which included the queen. At the close one of the visitors asked Malini to tell him how much money he had in his pockets. "That is easily done," replied the magician.
>
> To allow of no deception Malini was blindfolded, and at his request the visitor placed all the money on a table in full view of the spectators. There was a dead silence for a few seconds.
>
> "You are quite sure it is all on the table?" "Quite sure." "Then, sir, you have no money in your pockets." No one enjoyed this simple trick more than the queen.

The secret to Malini's success in London? He had "won his way by sheer force of manner," declared the *Penny Magazine*, "coupled with a skill at once remarkable, and, truth to tell, a trifle uncanny. He has no apparatus whatever—no concealed wire, batteries, or trick cabinets, and does his work in drawing-rooms with his audience around him."

That combination—a forceful personality and extraordinary sleight-of-hand skills—would serve him well during a lengthy career that never faltered, and that took him around the world. One of his last shows, in 1942, was at a magicians' club in Seattle. Years later, one of its members recalled the event:

> From the moment he began, you were struck by his personality. The magic was marvelous, but he was more so. His charming accent, the amusing way he used the language, and his infinite wit, captivated us all! Malini's remarkable personality almost overshadowed the magic. After all these years I can see him vividly while I've forgotten details of the tricks.

Malini's misuse of language was part of his appeal. The Katz family had immigrated to the U.S. from Galicia, when Max was a boy; and he never lost his accent. Indeed, he exaggerated it and made it a part of his stage persona. Malini played the part of a brash Eastern European Jew, whose English was imperfect and comical. It was replete with malapropisms, mispronunciations, and other lapses—most of them intentional. (Appearing before the Prince and Princess of Wales, for example, he had asked "Meeses Wales" to take a card.) Malini knew that this persona was one of the keys to his popularity. His son Ozzie once criticized him for his poor use of English. Malini told the youth: "I speak better English, you no eat."

No film footage of Malini performing is known to exist. But his hotel show has been described in detail. Typically, it took place on a wooden platform erected in the ballroom. On the platform was a table, furnished with decks of cards and a few commonplace items. There were also some potted plants that he had procured free of charge, having charmed the florist with an impromptu trick and tickets to the show. Selling tickets at the door was his wife Lizzie. A pianist was providing music.

When everyone had been seated, Malini emerged from a screened-off area that served as his dressing room. He was short (5′3″); portly (Malini enjoyed good food); and elegantly attired in a white suit. (Both onstage and offstage, he was a dapper dresser.) Malini greeted the audience, in his accented English. He told them that no elaborate paraphernalia—no fancy apparatus—would be used in his show. Nor, he said, did he require an assistant.

Then for two hours he entertained nonstop. (There were brief intermissions, during which he changed outfits—first into a black suit and cloak, then into a Chinese robe.) He did tricks with cards, coins, handkerchiefs, tumblers, cigars, a bowl of water. Each trick was skillfully executed and accompanied by a witty patter. The highlight of the show was his Blindfolded Card Stabbing routine. And Malini always brought a member of the audience onto the platform, and bit off one of his buttons.

His performances at the homes of the wealthy—about half-an-hour in length—were even less elaborate. The guests were entertained with close-up magic that was all the more amazing for its intimacy. For these engagements he needed little more than a deck of cards. The story is told of Malini's arrival at a mansion one evening, carrying only a small bag. It contained everything he needed for his performance.

"But where is your show?" the hostess asked him. She was dismayed, having expected a magician with a carload of props and an assistant or two. After all, his fee was sizeable.

Malini replied, "Madam, I am the show."

Professor Neuman

A century ago, on the lower level of Grand Central Station, there was a restaurant called Mendel's. It was open all night, and was famous for its oyster stew. E. B. White, the essayist, had fond memories of dining there as a youth:

> And when we reached Grand Central, we went in a swarm to Mendel's restaurant for dinner, and Mr. Mendel himself...would come to our table to greet us and we would all jump to our feet, including Mother, at the excitement of being recognized and singled out in a great public dining hall by the proprietor himself. Then the boarding of the fashionable train, and the green delights of compartments and drawing rooms and uppers and lowers.

Popular with travelers, Mendel's was especially favored by vaudevillians. Coming in late from shows in outlying towns, they would meet there to eat and socialize. Among them was a mindreader known as Professor Neuman.

To publicize his act, Neuman decided to do a "blindfolded walk" (as it was called by mentalists). And he would do it in Grand Central Station, that most public of places. The scenario was this: A committee of reputable persons would be formed. At some place of business inside the station, they would leave a package. Neuman would be blindfolded. And by reading their minds, he would lead the committeemen directly to the package.

The key to performing this feat was a technique called the "blindfold peek," or "beating the blindfold." Pretending to secure it, or to make it more comfortable, the mentalist would adjust his blindfold—until he was able to peek downwards. Once he could see, various schemes became possible. He could, for example, walk along a street, flanked by a pair of committeemen who are told to think of the package's location.

> Upon nearing a corner, you peer down from beneath the blindfold to stop at the proper spot. Then you simply wait, motionless, telling your companions to keep concentrating.... So while you wait, you keep looking down from under the blindfold, watching the feet of the committeemen. No matter how calm and immobile they try to be, in surprisingly few moments, one or both of the committeemen will turn his foot in the direction you are to take. In effect, intense concentration produces a subconscious reaction, in which the man literally, yet inadvertently, points out your path. The moment that you get that wigwag, you go, drawing your companions with you, much to their amazement.*

Using a method such as this, Neuman could locate the hidden package; and the publicity would be a boost to his career. So he embarked upon the stunt. The newspapers were notified; and a committee—composed of reputable persons who could not be accused of collusion—was formed. And on the scheduled day, Professor Neuman strode into Grand Central Station. He was formally dressed, as if for a performance at a theatre. Awaiting him were the committeemen, along with reporters and photographers.

The station was bustling with travelers. Curious as to what was happening, a crowd of spectators gathered. Neuman addressed them, describing his psychic powers and the feat he was about to attempt. At some place of business inside the station, he explained, the committeemen had left a package. The name of the business had been disclosed to no one. But he was going to locate the package—by reading the minds of the committeemen.

---

* These instructions are found in *Dunninger's Secrets* (1974) by mentalist Joseph Dunninger (as told to Walter Gibson)—my source for the story of Professor Neuman. In retelling a story that Dunninger no doubt embellished, I have taken the liberty of further embellishing it, with probable details.

They blindfolded him. Complaining that it was painful, Neuman adjusted the blindfold. And flanked by committeemen, one on each arm, he announced that he was ready. (Indeed he was—he could now see downwards!)

Neuman may have been prepared to take cues from their feet. But he had a different scheme in mind. It was simple yet daring, and part of the standard repertoire of a mind-reader.

As the committeemen held his arms and prepared to be led through the station, the blindfolded mentalist asked if there was a telephone directory handy. Yes, he was told—on a stand beside a nearby phone booth. (Actually, he already knew this, having purposely positioned himself in the vicinity of the booth.) They guided Neuman to the directory. Squeezed between the two men, he asked them to open it—to the page with the listing for that place of business. One of them did so; and Neuman asked him to point to the name. The purpose of doing so, he explained, was to insure that they were thinking of—were *concentrating* on—the location of the package.

The committeeman pointed to the name in the directory. Neuman clutched his head. He was struggling to read their minds, he told them. But in fact, he was peering down past his nose, at the name of the business. It was MENDEL'S.

Armed with this knowledge, and privately triumphant, Neuman led the committeemen through the station. On purpose he kept bumping into things, to give the impression of being securely blindfolded and unable to see. To prolong the suspense, he took an indirect route to the restaurant. He exited the station and walked toward Lexington Avenue. Dunninger describes the havoc that ensued:

> Watching his own feet, he worked his way back to Forty-second Street and sped his pace as he practically dragged the committeemen into Mendel's, with reporters, photographers, and some of the crowd following. Next, he was blundering among the tables, shoving chairs aside or looking under them, and when the committeemen began steering him toward the door, he went behind the cashier's

counter, poking underneath for the all-important package. When it wasn't there, he knew it must be in the kitchen, so he headed that way, pushing the manager aside when he tried to raise a protest.

By the time the professor was rummaging among the pots and pans, the police arrived and hauled him out through the back door. He had lost the committee somewhere along the way, and he hadn't found the package.

He hadn't found it because it wasn't there. *He had gone to the wrong Mendel's.*

When Grand Central opened in 1913, a man named William Mendel was awarded three concessions: the main restaurant; a candy shop; and the parcel room for the station. For many

years he ran these businesses. All of them were known as Mendel's.

The committeemen had checked the package at the parcel room. But Professor Neuman—*mis*reading their minds—had gone instead to the restaurant.

•

Professor Neuman is remembered for his fiasco at Grand Central Station. Dunninger describes him as "a small-time vaudeville mind reader who...worked blindfolded, mostly with stacked decks." Born in Russia, Dietrich Neuman claimed to be a genuine psychic, and on several occasions offered to help the police solve a crime. (The offers were ignored.) He was also a daredevil: in 1902 at a fair in Minnesota, he performed a balloon ascension and parachute leap. Little else is known about him. But his handbill advertised that the "Australian Fire Queen" (presumedly a fire-eater) traveled with him.*

---

* Professor Neuman is not to be confused with Newmann the Great, another mentalist of the same era. Newmann the Great, who billed himself as "The World's Greatest Mind Reader" (as did Professor Neuman) and as "America's Foremost Hypnotist," was popular in rural areas. He performed in small towns, either at the local opera house or in a tent, and is remembered for his "famous Blindfold Drive," in which he drove a team of horses through the streets.

The Great Lester

"THE BATTLE OF THE LESTERS," AS THE *Evening Sun* dubbed it, was waged in the Circuit Court of Baltimore, in April 1943. Harry Lester, a ventriloquist, had brought suit against Noel Lester, a magician. Both had been performing as The Great Lester. But Harry claimed to have exclusive rights to the name. A month earlier he had petitioned the court, asking that Noel be restrained from calling himself The Great Lester. The two men were appearing now before Judge Edwin Dickerson.

Harry's lawsuit had been prompted by his reception at the 21 Club, a Baltimore nightclub, upon arriving for an engagement. To his dismay, he found that his picture was not posted with those of the other performers. He had been dropped, explained the manager, because another Great Lester was appearing at the Maryland Theatre, a local vaudeville house. "We didn't know who was who and what was what," the manager told Harry, "or which Lester we were getting." Or maybe there was only one Lester, he insinuated, who was trying to two-time the club.

The misunderstanding was resolved; and Harry performed as a ventriloquist at the 21 Club. But he was furious. For he had encountered this fellow before. At a New York theatre in 1933, a magician named Noel Lester had billed himself as The Great Lester. Harry had filed suit, claiming to be the original—the actual—the one and only—Great Lester. Before the case could be tried, their attorneys had met and reached a settlement. It was agreed that only Harry would use the name.

Then, in Detroit eight years later, their paths had again crossed—and Noel was still billing himself as The Great Lester! But before Harry could take legal action, the magician had fled the state.

This time, in Baltimore, Harry had acted quickly. And

the matter was about to be adjudicated in Judge Dickerson's courtroom.

If priority turned out to be the deciding factor, Harry—who had begun calling himself The Great Lester earlier than Noel—would prevail. On the other hand, his real name was not Lester. He had been born Marian Czajkowski, in the Polish town of Lobens. (The composer Tchaikovsky, he claimed, was a relative.) The family had emigrated to America in 1880, when Marian was a year old; and he had grown up in Chicago. As a teenager he took up magic, busking on street corners and performing in beer gardens. Marian wanted to become a magician, not a shoemaker like his father. But his parents enrolled him in St. Mary's College, a seminary in Kentucky. They were hoping he would enter the priesthood. Instead, he dropped out during his first year and joined the Hummel & Hamilton Circus.

At first he labored as a roustabout, driving stakes and helping to raise the tent. Eventually he was promoted to clown. And finally he became Kaloofra the Magician, performing in a sideshow tent. He was ballyhooed as either Kaloofra the Hindoo Magician or Kaloofra the Arabian Magician—depending on which costume he had donned that day.

From the circus he moved on to carnivals and dime museums, still doing magic as Kaloofra. Summers were spent in a sideshow at Coney Island. During this period he also performed as a mindreader, a fire-eater, and a contortionist. And then, at the age of 23, he found his true calling: ventriloquism.

Using a dummy (or "figure," as he insisted upon calling it), he developed a ventriloquist act. He called his dummy Frank Byron Jr. And he adopted a stage name: Harry Lester. Almost immediately, he found work in vaudeville. With Frank Byron Jr. perched on his knee, Harry performed at theatres on the lesser circuits. He also helped with props and distributed handbills for the shows. Traveling by train from engagement to engagement, The Great Lester, as he billed himself, stayed at cheap hotels and theatrical boarding houses.

Harry and Maggie (the first of his wives) had based themselves in New York, where most booking took place. But generally they were on the road. Finally, in 1909, Harry broke into the "big-time," with a booking at the Alhambra in New York. In a review of his act, *Variety* reported that "The Great Lester was a big laughing and applause hit." And it offered this advice:

> Anybody with "The Great" tacked upon his billing name is expected to be "good." So The Great Lester is good, very good, as a ventriloquist, and might be better liked even without "The Great" hanging about, entirely unnecessary.

Harry (who ignored that advice) went on to appear at Keith & Proctor's Fifth Avenue Theatre. And he began to travel on the two major circuits, the Keith and the Orpheum. He had become a headliner, the pinnacle of success for a vaudevillian.*

Harry became the most popular ventriloquist on the American stage. And there was more to come. In 1910 he crossed the Atlantic for a tour that would take him as far as St. Petersburg. In London, at the Hippodrome, he shared the bill with Sarah Bernhardt. A review noted that "the Great Lester, an American ventriloquist who opened at the London Hippodrome Monday, easily established himself as

* A vaudeville show generally had nine acts on its bill. A "dumb act," such as acrobats or trained dogs, opened the show, while latecomers were still finding seats. The "deuce" spot was in front of the curtain, as the stage was being set for the third act. (Performing in front of the curtain was known as "in one.") Next came the "flash act": a major production number, such as a short play, with sets and a large cast. Another in-one act followed—a comic, a singer, a juggler. The coveted fifth spot was for the second headliner. Then came an intermission, for the sale of refreshments. The sixth spot was often a dumb act. The seventh was another full-stage production. And the eighth spot was reserved for the top headliner. The show closed with a dumb act, as the audience began to leave.

favorite." At the Alhambra he was advertised as "America's premier ventriloquist." And Harry performed for King George V.

His act was twelve minutes long. He sat at a table between the curtain and the footlights, with Frank Byron Jr. on his knee. Frank was a wise-cracking youth; and Harry was his straight man. Frank seemed weirdly alive as he joked, sang, and even yodeled. At one point Harry would walk down the aisle with him; and Frank would converse with members of the audience. Harry Lester was not the first ventriloquist to perform with a dummy. But so successful was he that having one became standard practice. And Frank Byron Jr., brash and disrespectful, would serve as a model for the dummies who came after him.

Harry was famous for a particular feat. He would puff on a cigarette, and down a full glass of supposed whiskey, *while Frank talked continuously.* It seemed impossible that Harry was providing the voice; yet he was. One night, as a prank, members of the orchestra substituted real whiskey for the colored water in the glass. (Such pranks were a vaudeville tradition.) As Harry chatted with Frank, the musicians

waited expectantly for him to start drinking and choke. They were taken aback when he downed the whiskey yet showed no signs of distress. Frank, however, began to sputter, choke, and go into spasms! Bested by Harry's coolness, the musicians rose and applauded him.

For more than a decade The Great Lester was in demand as a ventriloquist; and he prospered. But his career eventually went into decline. His act had become outdated. For lengthy periods he performed little or not at all. His second wife had left him; and Harry fell into a debilitating depression. Moreover, vaudeville itself was in decline, due to the popularity of movies and radio. Vaudeville theatres were being converted into movie theatres. Live acts were still being booked, but often as mere accompaniment to a film. In 1929 Harry's contracts were cancelled—and he was suspended from the Orpheum circuit—after walking out of an engagement. And later that year the stock market crashed, wiping out his savings.

But perhaps the cruelest blow was a movie called *The Great Gabbo.* It starred Erich von Stroheim as a ventriloquist who abuses his girlfriend-assistant; has an unhealthy relationship with his dummy (whom he treats as a person); and finally loses his mind. The Great Gabbo—who has the unique ability to smoke and drink while throwing his voice—was clearly based on The Great Lester. The film was even advertised as having a factual basis. Harry claimed it was libelous and initiated a lawsuit. And he probably would have prevailed, had the production company not folded to escape liability.

Harry Lester had become a has-been—a vaudeville headliner who now barely eked out a living. He was largely forgotten, by both the public and his fellow entertainers. But then he made a comeback of sorts—thanks to a journalistic blunder by Ed Sullivan.

Sullivan was a syndicated columnist (and later a television host) who reported on show business. The latest doings on Broadway were his specialty. In his column for January 6, 1937, Sullivan ill-advisedly wrote the following:

> Every time I see one of these ventriloquists, I think of the most famous of them all. He used a certain dummy figure for years, finally becoming convinced that the dummy, instead of being inanimate, was really alive. Performers used to hear the ventriloquist bitterly abusing the dummy in his dressing room, claiming that he was laying down in the act. A few months later, the ventriloquist went violently insane, tore the dummy to pieces, was committed to the insane asylum. That was The Great Lester, one of the higher-priced vaudeville acts.

He had confused Harry with the fictional Gabbo.

Ed Sullivan soon received a call from Harry, who was living in Detroit. The Great Lester assured the columnist that he had neither gone insane nor been committed to an asylum. Moreover, he intended to sue for libel. Realizing that his error could prove costly, Sullivan begged Harry to meet with him before taking legal action. Harry agreed to a meeting.

Sullivan took the next train to Detroit, apologized to Harry, and offered him a deal. If Harry would agree not to sue, Sullivan would sponsor his comeback on Broadway and provide him with publicity.

Harry took the deal; and that spring he moved back to New York. Accompanying him was his third wife, a graphologist whose stage name was Eedah, and whom he had met while playing a club in Detroit. Eedah billed herself as "The Psychic Wonder of the Age." They rented an apartment in the Bronx.

In May *Variety* reported:

> The Great Lester, once the No. 1 ventriloquist in vaude, is currently making a New York comeback at the Wivel, Swedish restaurant-nitery. He hasn't shown in N.Y. for around seven years.
>
> Besides the Wivel date, Great Lester is auditioning for a spot on Fred Allen's air program, with negotiations now on for the ventriloquist act to follow the Swedish eatery date with an engagement in the French Casino's cocktail room.
>
> Billy Jackson is agenting.

Harry remained at the Wivel for twenty-one weeks. But his comeback proved to be limited. For the next six years he worked sporadically. Based in the Bronx, he traveled to whatever gigs he could get. Sometimes he and Eedah were booked at the same club.

Then, in March of 1943, Harry took the train to Baltimore, for an engagement at the 21 Club. And his path crossed once again with that of Noel Lester.

Less is known about the other Great Lester, whom Harry would be battling in court. He was born in 1894 in St. Louis. Unlike Harry, who had dropped out of college to join the circus, Noel had grown up in a circus. His father (according to his testimony during the trial) was a magician who had called himself The Great Lester. Both father and son had been magicians with the Sells-Floto circus. During World War I Noel had served in the Navy. Since then, he had been performing—in tents, vaudeville houses, and movie theatres—as The Great Lester, having inherited the name from his father. To publicize himself, he would arrive in a town and do a blindfolded drive—weaving his way through traffic by hunches, he claimed, that were "projected from the minds of the spectators who line the street." (More likely, he peeked.)

Noel publicized his show with the usual puffery. This notice (clearly a ready-made write-up from his pressbook) appeared in the Clovis (New Mexico) *News-Journal*:

> The Great Lester, world's foremost master of magic and his company, has been booked to appear at the Lyceum theatre this coming Thursday at midnight. The Great Lester is said to be one of the finest masters of ledgerdemain [sic] in the world and has been the center of comment of the most skeptical critics who were forced to admit that his great array of baffling illusions and ghostly effects were beyond solution....
>
> The Great Lester is the only magician today who is presenting a real ghost seance in which attempts are made to get messages for members of the audience from the world beyond. You will also see Lester's baffling Hindu levitation

> effect with a young lady. In addition to the personal performance of the master magician there will also be on the program wire walking, juggling, singing, dancing, etc.

So—did Harry have exclusive rights to the name The Great Lester? Or was Noel also entitled? Judge Dickerson would decide. And in a fifteen-page Memorandum, the judge would review the testimony and explain his decision.*

In a Baltimore courtroom, each of the two made a case for his rights to the name. In the Memorandum Judge Dickerson reviews Noel's testimony:

> The defendant testified that he was doing magic with his father in a circus side show in 1907, and that they were known as The Big and Little Lesters, and that the banner on the side show bore the device, "The Great Lester, Magician"; that with the exception of one year, when he played as The Variety Boy on circuit, he has played in theatres as The Great Lester, the Magician, since 1919; that with one exception, about a year ago, he has never played a night club; that he knew his father used the name The Great Lester, the Magician, as far back as 1903. His performances in Baltimore as The Great Lester, the Magician, were at the Garden Theatre twenty years ago, the Hippodrome in 1933, the State Theatre in 1935, and at the Maryland Theatre in the current year. He last played in New York in 1936, and then toured the South, West, Hawaii and Australia as The Great Lester, the Magician. He testified that he first heard of the plaintiff in 1933 when sued in New York.

The judge notes that the defendant "disclaimed all knowledge of the plaintiff's claim to fame under the sobriquet of The Great Lester, denies that he has pirated the plaintiff's title, and, on the contrary, avers that he is The Great Lester."

---

* I came upon this Memorandum (which sparked my interest in the Lesters) at the Enoch Pratt Free Library in Baltimore. A legal document typed on onionskin paper, it had been donated to the library by Judge Dickerson.

Also taking the stand was Diane Lester, described by the *Evening Sun* as Noel's "attractive black-haired wife." She testified that she had first witnessed him perform as The Great Lester at a Boston theatre in 1924. And three Baltimore magicians testified that Noel had been calling himself The Great Lester for many years.

But Harry's claim was no less persuasive. Judge Dickerson notes that the plaintiff "testified that he first used the name of The Great Lester in 1904." (That is to say, fifteen years before Noel first used it, though a year after Noel's father.) And the judge continues:

> The plaintiff alleged in his bill that he is an actor of international fame and is known in the theatrical profession as the world's foremost artistic ventriloquist, that he has received acclaim from foreign and domestic rulers and statesmen and has performed in nearly all the leading theatres at home and abroad; that he has been known as The Great Lester in his theatrical career, has built up an enviable reputation under that name, has performed with many famous actors and actresses and has been featured in leading newspapers and magazines as the world's greatest ventriloquist, has received as high as $1,500 for weekly performances, and that by 1926 he had amassed a large fortune and had retired to live on it, lost his fortune and was compelled to return to the theatre for a living; that in 1933, he discovered the defendant had pirated his goodwill and was appearing under the name of The Great Lester on the New York stage.

Noel's attorney agreed that Harry had built an enviable reputation under the name. But that reputation was *as a ventriloquist,* he argued. And since Noel was a magician, the two men followed different professions. Thus, they were not in competition with one another; and his client could not be accused of infringing on Harry's reputation.

When Harry took the stand, he denied being solely a ventriloquist—he was a magician as well, he insisted. "He alleged," reports Judge Dickerson, "that his artistic ability is not confined to ventriloquism, but that he also enjoys a world-wide reputation as a magician." And while admitting that he hadn't billed himself as a magician since years before, Harry claimed to frequently include magic in his act.

Noel's attorney asked Harry to prove he was a magician by doing the coin-tray trick. And he handed Harry a silver tray containing some coins. Harry refused to take it and became angry. "I don't need that tray—that's junk to me!" Harry complained to the judge: "He wants to find out my trick."

Judge Dickerson tried to calm him down. But Harry was agitated. He insisted that the tray wasn't a real coin tray. "I can't tell why it's not, because it's a secret." A real magician, explained Harry, needed preparation and his own special equipment. And indicating Noel, he said: "Of course, there are some magicians who just go to a magic store—" The judge interrupted and told him to stop.

Noel was no more respectful of his rival. At one point he interrupted Harry's testimony with a booming laugh—a breach of decorum for which he was reprimanded by the judge. And he drew attention to the fact that Harry's original name was not Lester.

The trial lasted several days, drawing the press and providing entertainment for spectators. A memorable moment came late in the trial. A magician named Walter Lester took the stand and said that he too had been known as The Great Lester. The defense was offering him as evidence for the non-exclusivity of the name. Judge Dickerson reports:

> Walter J. Lester testified that he and his brother were known as The Great Lester as far back as 1900, and played under that name in that year in the capital of Lithuania; that the witness went by this name from fifteen to twenty-five years ago, and was billed as such in minor magic eighteen years ago. He testified that he met the defendant's father twenty-five years ago in a small town in the South, when their respective shows converged, and that they both were recognized as The Great Lester in their respective shows.

Thus, there had been (at least) five Great Lesters: Harry,

Noel, Noel's father, Walter, and Walter's brother!

Judge Dickerson pondered the testimonies; examined the exhibits (contracts, newspaper clippings); studied opinions in similar cases; and arrived at a decision. He rejected Harry's claim of exclusivity, and refused to grant an injunction or to award damages. The judge based his decision, he explained, on three considerations:

(1) Multiple individuals had performed professionally, and over a significant period of time, as The Great Lester.

(2) The litigants were not in direct competition, as one was a ventriloquist ("the high note of his career has been ventriloquism, which has sounded and resounded throughout this country and abroad"), while the other was a magician ("using three trucks to convey his ten tons of magical equipment throughout every State in the Union"). As for Harry's claim that he was also a magician, it was untenable:

> He declined to perform magic at the trial or to touch proffered magical paraphernalia, which left the Court under the impression that, while he was an excellent ventriloquist, as he demonstrated at the trial, he could not give an equivalent performance in magic and the conclusion of the Court is that magic is not a strong role with the plaintiff.

And Harry himself had confirmed that the roles were distinct. "He testified that his occupation since 1892 has been ventriloquism and magic, thus differentiating in his own mind these two fields of entertainment."

(3) Harry had failed to pursue his claim in a timely fashion. This was the deciding factor for Judge Dickerson. The judge applied a legal concept called laches—a statute of limitations. Harry had waited too long before filing the present suit. He had "slept" on his rights:

> For nearly seven years after the intended Michigan suit, and for nearly ten years after the institution of the New York suit, the defendant has used the name of The Great Lester, as a magician, unmolested....It seems entirely clear that the plaintiff has been guilty of laches, and cannot in

> this suit assert rights, if he once had them, on which he has slumbered so long. Vigilantibus non dormientibus equitas subvenit ["equity aids the vigilant, not the negligent"] seems definitely applicable to the facts of this case.

The judge's decision? "The Court has reached the conclusion that the plaintiff does not have the paramount right to the use of the name The Great Lester." And Judge Dickerson dismissed the suit.

Harry was deeply disappointed. All that remained of his days as a headliner was that name; and he could no longer call it his own. He stayed in Baltimore for a while, having found work at other clubs, then returned to the Bronx. Soon thereafter, he and Eedah went on tour, playing nightclubs and fairs. But as bookings became less frequent, they realized that their careers in show business were ending.

The tour ended in San Francisco; and they decided to stay there. Harry found work as a handyman for an antique dealer, and later as a car upholsterer, and collected Social Security. On rare occasions he performed. Eedah opened a dress shop. But the strains on their marriage had grown; and they eventually divorced. Eedah went back to Minnesota. Harry took a Greyhound bus to Los Angeles, and rented an apartment over a hardware store in Hollywood.

And he embarked now upon a new career, as a teacher of ventriloquism. The front room of his apartment became a studio, with full-length mirrors. Taped to the walls were glossy photographs of vaudevillians he had known. Novice ventriloquists came to him for lessons; and Harry passed on his knowledge of the art. He taught them voice technique and figure manipulation. There were breathing exercises, whispering exercises, lip exercises. "It was an amazing experience," one of his students would recall:

> Lester had very precise and specific ways he approached teaching. He was in his seventies at the time and was a patient and gracious instructor. He was a perfectionist, but in a gentle way. We would practice for hours at a time.... When we would take a break, Lester would perform and

> teach us magic tricks. I still do his cut and restored string for my grandkids, exactly as Lester had taught.

The students provided Harry with both a professional and a social life. He welcomed them to his studio. And once a month, meetings of the Los Angeles Society of Magicians were held there.

And he gave one final performance, on the television show *You Asked for It.* A viewer who had once seen "a famous ventriloquist" drink and vocalize simultaneously, asked to see that feat again. With Broadway Eddie on his knee, Harry performed it. (Frank Byron Jr. had retired, Harry explained, and Broadway Eddie was his successor.)

He died on July 14, 1956. The *Los Angeles Times* reported:

> The Great Lester—Ventriloquist Harry Lester—died yesterday at General Hospital at the age of 77.... For the past decade, Lester had operated a studio at 5540 Hollywood Blvd. He was world traveled and at one time an internationally famous entertainer.

Blackstone

On January 2, 1963, the Magic Castle opened its doors. Perched on a hillside in Hollywood, the 22-room mansion—occupied originally by a wealthy banker, then made into a home for the elderly, then divided into small apartments—had been converted into a private club for magicians. About fifty adepts had signed up for membership. Those who entered on that first day were greeted by a work-in-progress; for restoration of the maze-like interior was still in its early stages. But the Main Lounge was ready for use: plush chairs, and six stools at the bar, awaited occupants. The Close-up Gallery was available as a venue for magic. The Invisible Irma Room was presided over by a ghostly pianist, who played any tune requested.

And of the spaces that had been completed, none was more welcoming than the Blackstone Room. Named in honor of the celebrated magician, it contained baize-covered tables, for the presentation of card tricks or other close-up magic. It also contained, on that inaugural day, Blackstone himself.

Harry Blackstone had retired in 1959, after an illustrious and lucrative career; and with his third wife Betsy, had settled in Hollywood. Their apartment on Sycamore Avenue happened to be two blocks away from the turreted mansion that would become the Magic Castle. When the club opened, he was urged to make himself at home in the Blackstone Room. And he was pleased to do so, night after night. The room became his hangout. Members would find Blackstone seated in the chair that was reserved for him. As amiable as ever, he socialized with friends and admirers. He did card tricks for his fellow magicians, displaying a skill that was undiminished. He exchanged gossip. And he reminisced about the sixty years he had spent in show business.

During the early years of that career, he had struggled to make a name for himself as a magician—a name that kept changing. Born in 1885 and raised in Chicago, young Harry Boughton had been drawn to magic as a hobby. At sixteen he found employment in a woodworking shop. One of his assignments was to make trick boxes for a magic dealer; and the enterprising Harry made duplicates for his own use. He included them in the amateur performances he was giving at schools and churches.

Finally, he began to work professionally. With his brother Pete he formed a duo called The Two Franciscos. Their act consisted of Harry doing straight magic, while Pete, dressed as a clown, lampooned him. They performed at local theatres. Then, in 1910, an agent caught their act and booked the brothers on a vaudeville circuit. Rebranding themselves as Harry Bouton and Company, they began to travel out-of-state.

The buffoonery was eventually dropped. Pete assumed other roles, as Harry became a solo performer. And the act kept evolving. In 1913 a magician known as The Great Albini died in his hotel room after a show. His paraphernalia was put up for sale; and Harry purchased it. He also hired Albini's mechanic, and took on a female assistant—the first in his bevy of "Gorgeous Girls."

The company now numbered four. Together they traveled the circuit from theatre to theatre. And work was plentiful in that heyday of vaudeville. Curiously, Harry performed under a succession of names. These included LeRoy Boughton, Mr. Quick, Maximillian, C. Porter Norton (substituting for the actual Norton), Harry Careejo, and The Great Stanley. But his career reached a new level in 1915—the year he began performing as Fredrik the Great.

A magician by that name had gone broke and been unable to pay for the lithographed posters that had been printed for him. Emblazoned with the name "Fredrik the Great," these posters depicted elaborate illusions and were vibrant with color. Harry purchased them from the printer at a greatly reduced rate. Neither he nor his show bore a resemblance to what was pictured on the posters. (Fredrik had worn old-fashioned knee breeches; Harry performed in evening dress.) But he began using the posters, and calling himself Fredrik the Great.

By 1917 Harry—as Fredrik the Great—was presenting a full-evening show, with large-scale illusions and multiple assistants. Among those assistants was Inez Nourse, a vaudevillian who billed herself as "The Little Banjophiend"—and to whom Harry would soon be wed. She had joined the show while it was playing in Michigan. Inez served as music director, rehearsing the house orchestra, and also provided a musical interlude on her banjo. Other female assistants were vanishing, levitating, or hopping out of boxes. Pete was the carpenter for the show, building props and sets. And things were going well for Fredrik the Great and company, when history intervened.

In April of that year, the U.S. entered the war against Germany. Suddenly, anything associated with Germany—even sauerkraut!—was deemed to be unpatriotic. A performer called Fredrik the Great was presumed to be German. And while Harry had established a reputation under it, the name was now a liability. Ticket sales declined sharply. A new stage name, he realized, had to be adopted. But what should it be?

The inspiration for it came after a show one night, as he and Inez were taking a walk. They passed a billboard that advertised Blackstone cigars. "That's it!" cried Inez. "That's the name." Suggestive of a mystic stone—a wonder-working gem—it seemed perfect for a magician.

Soon thereafter, the show opened at the Grand Theatre in Tiffin, Ohio. It now featured "Blackstone the Great." Overnight, Fredrik had vanished; and Blackstone had replaced him. It was a transformation worthy of a wizard.

Performing as Blackstone the Great, Harry enjoyed a sudden rise to prominence. It was as if the name, like the gem, possessed a supernatural power, and had brought him success. Bookings abounded; audiences flocked to see him. And by 1920 he could afford his own lithographed posters. In garish splendor they advertised Blackstone's "Oriental Nights" and his "Congress of Spooks." They proclaimed him to be "The World's Master Magician." And they showed him performing alongside Mephistopheles. (It was as if he made a deal with the Devil!)

During the 1920s he became a leading name in vaudeville—a headliner. His acclaim grew, along with the size of his company. And when Howard Thurston died in 1936, Blackstone succeeded him as America's premier magician. The company toured with two versions of the show. One lasted fifty minutes, and could either share a stage with other acts or accompany a film. The other was an extravaganza that lasted two hours.

Then war came again; and Blackstone volunteered his services. During the war he gave more than a thousand performances at military bases. His show, with its mystifying illusions and costumed showgirls, was a hit with soldiers. And in 1947 he returned to theatrical touring—the last magician with a full-evening show. (Blackstone was billing himself now as "The Last of the Great Magicians.") Such was his fame that he continued to draw large audiences. Finally, in 1955, he gave his final show and dissolved the company.

The contents of the show had changed from year to year. But a number of illusions had become part of his standard repertoire. The evening might begin, or end, with The Enchanted Garden. Bouquets of flowers were magically produced until the stage overflowed with them. There was The Floating Light Bulb, his signature illusion. The Vanishing Bird Cage, in which Blackstone—surrounded by children from the audience—held in plain sight a cage with a canary, and made it disappear. The Levitation of Princess Karnac. And The Sepoy Mutiny, in which Blackstone was captured by rebels and lashed across the mouth of a cannon. The fuse was lit by a bearded Indian. There was a fiery explosion; and when the smoke cleared, Blackstone had vanished. Then the Indian removed his turban, beard, and robe—and it was Blackstone!*

---

* How had this transposition been effected? As the rebels milled about the captured Blackstone, a dummy was substituted for him

The big production numbers, with their elaborate sets, alternated with simple tricks that could be performed in front of the curtain. This allowed the sets to be changed without a pause in the magic. Among these tricks was The Disappearing Watch. Blackstone would descend from the stage; ask for a volunteer with a watch; and lead the obliging member of the audience up onto the stage. Blackstone folded a sheet of paper around the watch. When he unfolded it, the watch was gone. Then he wadded up the paper and made it too disappear. (It was simply tossed over the volunteer's head, to the amusement of the audience.) Next, Blackstone—who was skilled at picking pockets—handed the volunteer his wallet. Finally, a loaf of bread, freshly baked at a local bakery, was brought on stage. Blackstone cut it open and extracted a bottle. He broke open the bottle, to reveal a live rabbit. And tied to the rabbit's neck was the volunteer's watch.*

The Blackstone show had a mesmerizing flow to it. It was a non-stop ride of tricks and illusions—a cavalcade of

---

and lashed to the cannon. When the cannon was fired, the dummy —under cover of the smoke—was collapsed and drawn into the barrel. Meanwhile, Blackstone had donned a turban, beard, and robe and taken the place of the Indian.

* On one occasion, during the fifties, that volunteer was my father. The Blackstone show, in its final days, was playing the Hanna Theatre in Cleveland; and my father took my brother and me to see it. I was nine years old; my brother was seven. We were seated near the front; and I remember Blackstone stopping beside my father—who had raised his hand to volunteer—and speaking with him. Then, unbelievably, our father left us and followed Blackstone up onto the stage. When the trick was over, he returned to his seat with gifts: a six-pack of 7-Up (it had been magically produced) and that loaf of bread.

Why did Blackstone select my father? Probably because of the two boys who were sitting with him. From years of experience, Blackstone knew that a family man was unlikely to be a troublemaker and would cooperate. And on stage, my father told me years later, Blackstone had whispered to him, asking him to go along with the trick.

magical effects, accompanied by music, that were baffling and compelling. Much of its success was due to the personality of Blackstone. He had a winning manner, a commanding stage presence, and a showmanship that few other magicians could match. Daniel Waldron, author of *Blackstone: A Magician's Life* (1999), describes him coming onto the stage:

> His powerful face, large penetrating eyes, beetling brow, dramatic shock of hair, arms poised at his sides as though ready to grapple with unseen forces—these plus a masterful voice that carried unamplified and seemingly without effort to the uppermost balcony—all these seized the imagination at once. And when, without a moment's pause, he tossed his white gloves into the air where they turned into a fluttering dove, well...could you doubt for one moment you were in the presence of strange powers?

He was always elegantly attired, in evening dress. Yet that formality was tempered with an amiable disposition. Some magicians affected a satanic air; Blackstone was warm, friendly, and good-humored. Occasionally, he even added a cowboy hat to his white tie and tails. Usually, though, he was bare-headed. And displayed was that distinctive shock of hair—those layered locks that were his trademark look. Mephistopheles had his red cap and feather; Blackstone had his hair.

Harry Blackstone had a personal magnetism that drew and riveted audiences. It also inspired loyalty among the thirty or so members of his company. This troupe of vaudevillians were constantly on the road together, traveling by train; and they became a close-knit family, with Blackstone (the Boss, as he was called) as paterfamilias. There were the showgirls—female assistants chosen for their looks and size. (They had to be pretty, but also small enough to fit into boxes and hidden compartments.) And the male assistants, who performed various tasks on stage and were costumed as bellhops. (The showgirls were more scantily clad.) And the stagehands, who were under the direction of Pete Bouton, Harry's brother. In their original act Pete had been the clown; now he was the show's mechanic and carpenter. He also supervised the unpacking and repacking of the crates that held the props, scenery, and lighting equipment for the show. These, along with animals in cages, were transported in a special, double-length baggage car. One of the crates was his portable workshop. It contained tools for cutting trap doors, repairing props, and dealing with any mechanical problem that might arise. In a memoir of her three years as a showgirl in the company, Adele Friel Rhindress describes Pete's role:

> The Blackstone show remained a double act. Each brother had to rely on the other's abilities. Harry called Pete "the mainspring of my watch" and, as far as I could see, that was absolutely true. The show as I knew it could not have gone on without Pete.
>
> Onstage, Blackstone commanded the attention and interest of the audience. Backstage, Pete Bouton was in command. He was our "everything" man, responsible for every piece of physical equipment in the show.
>
> When we were on the road, Pete made sure that all the orange-painted crates, along with his fire-engine red workshop on wheels, were transported from the train and loaded into the theater....
>
> Pete kept everything in proper working order. If a prop or illusion needed to be repaired, his portable workshop was at the ready. (*Memoirs of an Elusive Moth: Disappearing Nightly with Harry Blackstone and His Show of 1001 Wonders,* 2011)

And Pete was part of another duo: his wife Millie was the wardrobe mistress. At each theatre she would unpack the wardrobe trunks; set up racks of costumes in the wings; and supervise the frequent changes. She also served as a surrogate mother for the younger showgirls.

For nine months of the year, the company traveled from booking to booking. They slept in Pullman cars or in local hotels. They ate together, joked together, performed together. And they shared the vicissitudes of an itinerant life. There were rivalries, disappointments, and disputes. But there was also a strong sense of camaraderie. And during the summer that bond intensified. For most of the company spent the summer together on Blackstone Island.

Before the advent of air-conditioning, vaudeville theatres closed during the summer; and performers dispersed, until the theatres re-opened in the fall. But the Blackstone company stayed together and headed for their summer quarters, on an island of the St. Joseph River, near Colon, Michigan. In 1926 Blackstone had been performing in the area; and taken with the rural scenery, had purchased the island. Thereafter, the company spent their summers on what became known as Blackstone Island.

The island had come with a frame house, a barn, and fisherman's cottages. Harry and Inez took up residence in the house; while others moved into a cottage or rented a room in town. The barn served as a workshop and rehearsal space. Props were painted and repaired there; new illusions were built; and rehearsals were held for next season's show. (At the end of the summer, a final dress rehearsal—to which the townsfolk were invited—was held at the Opera House in Colon.) Much work took place on Blackstone Island. But so did swimming, fishing, and socializing. Each morning the entire company assembled in the house for breakfast; and each evening, re-assembled for dinner. Often joining them were guests: friends of Blackstone, or fellow magicians who had come to pay their respects.*

---

* Among the magicians who visited was Percy Abbott, an Australian. Initially, he and Blackstone hit it off together; and

The relaxed atmosphere provided a welcome break from the rigors of touring. It was also conducive to romance; and couples formed among the troupers. Nor was Blackstone himself immune to the charms of the showgirls. His straying was probably the cause of his divorce from Inez in 1930. Three years later he married Billie Matthews, one of the showgirls. Their wedding was held on the island.

They had one child: Harry Blackstone, Jr. The boy grew up amidst the bustle and communality of a theatrical company. He had made his first appearance on stage at the age of six months. The babysitter had failed to show up one night; and Billie—who had to burst through a map of the U.S., costumed as the Statue of Liberty—had done so holding her infant. As a youth, Harry was taught the basics of magic and included in the show. Yet his father discouraged him from pursuing a career in magic. Instead, he attended college and studied theatre. Then he worked as a radio announcer and a television producer—though occasionally as a magician.

But the name *Blackstone* had its hold on him. And when his father (who had been holding court daily at the Magic Castle) died in 1965, Harry began to get serious about magic. Perhaps he had needed to wait until *he,* and he alone, was Harry Blackstone. A break came when he was hired to be the magician for a show at Caesar's Palace in Las Vegas. Soon he was performing regularly, at nightclubs and hotels.

---

they founded the Blackstone Magic Company, for the manufacture of magical apparatus. Abbott took up residence in Colon. But he and Blackstone had a falling out; and Abbott continued the business on his own. The Abbott Magic Novelty Company, as he renamed it, would become a major supplier of apparatus.

Abbott married a local girl and settled permanently in Colon. And beginning in 1934, he sponsored an annual gathering of magicians in the town. Called Abbott's Magic Get-Together, it continues to attract magicians from around the world. They watch performances, attend lectures, buy tricks, and talk about magic. And some go out to the local cemetery, where Blackstone is buried, and pay homage to the master.

His talent was considerable; the name itself had a drawing power; and his rise was rapid. During the seventies he toured with his own full-evening show. It was a revival of the two-hour extravaganza—the type of show on which his father, a quarter-century earlier, had finally drawn the curtain. Included were The Floating Light Bulb, The Vanishing Bird Cage, and other illusions that the senior Blackstone had made famous. Drawing large audiences, the show played in 156 cities. In 1980 a musical version of it opened at the Majestic Theatre in New York. Titled *Blackstone!*, it became the longest-running magic show on Broadway. And like his namesake, Harry Blackstone, Jr. became the most acclaimed magician in America.

He had inherited his father's talent, genial personality,

and stage presence. But most of all, he had inherited that name. Suggestive of a wonder-working gem, it lent an aura to the father and son who bore it. Their magic seemed almost real.

The Banana Man

A MAGICIAN MAY PULL FROM HIS HAT A SUCCESSION OF items: a rabbit, a dove, a bottle of wine, a bouquet of flowers, colorful silks. Yet no less bountiful was the coat of the Banana Man—a cornucopia of a coat! Here is an account of what emerged from its pockets:

> Equipped with a pince-nez and violent red yarn wig and moustache, and dressed in his long purple coat, he walks on stage, unzips a banana equipped with a slide fastener, and throws the fruit away. He slips on the banana peel, and is forced to pull out [from a coat pocket] a pail and a long-handled mop to clean it up. Taking out some sheet music, he then produces a violin with which to play it. Pulling out a music stand and a stool from his coat, he settles down to work in earnest, all the while humming a lunatic little tune in falsetto. He becomes angry with the music, crumples it into a ball but has nowhere to put it. Out comes a waste basket. He solaces himself with an apple, but doesn't like it. Reaching into his coat he begins to pull out fruit—pineapples, bags of oranges and always more and more bananas. (Oden and Olivia Meeker, "Handyman Clown," *Mechanix Illustrated,* April 1945)

The list is incomplete. The Banana Man also produced, from his pockets, an oboe, a giant magnet, two watermelons, a dozen neckties, a box of cigars, mandolins, and more. As for those bananas, they emerged in bunches—dozens and dozens of bananas.

Who was this magical clown, who appeared on the vaudeville stage and later on television? Actually, two men performed as the Banana Man—one having inherited the act from the other. But the original Banana Man was a vaudevillian who called himself A. Robins.

Robins was born in 1886 (as Adolf Proper), the son of a

Viennese textile manufacturer. By his late teens he was performing in cabarets, as a quick-sketch artist. One of his "lightning pictures" was a seascape that he painted on a large paper hoop. Upon completing the painting, he dove through it. In addition to sketching, Robins impersonated a crazy music professor. He played on a collection of musical instruments, by humming and imitating their sounds. It was a unique form of ventriloquism. He concluded by smashing the instruments.

In 1912 Robins emigrated to the U.S. There he found work in vaudeville, as a novelty act. And he developed a new routine. Robins still simulated the sound of instruments; but he also pulled from his pockets a miscellany of items—most notably, bananas. Eventually, he was billed as "A. Robins the Banana Man."

The Banana Man would waddle on stage, pulling a trunk on wheels and cackling. (The trunk would serve as a receptacle for the emerging contents of his pockets.) With his zany hat, fright wig, fake eyebrows and mustache, and bulky overcoat, he was clearly a clown. He began by taking a prop oboe from his coat pocket and playing a tune on it—in reality, humming the tune. When he lowered the oboe from his mouth, to his surprise it continued to emit music. Next, he employed the same prop as a flute. Finally, he tossed it into the trunk.

There was a logic to what the Banana Man produced from his pockets. In need of a sheet of music, he pulled one out—along with a music stand. After crumpling up the music, he pulled out a waste basket. When he wanted to sit, out came a stool. When he craved a drink, a bottle and a glass. And when he was hungry, bunch after bunch of bananas! Finding these things in his pockets made him happy. The Banana Man would emit a screech of delight—a high-pitched "la la la la la, oooooh, wow!" Otherwise, he never spoke.*

In addition to his talents as a clown (and he was the highest-paid clown in vaudeville), Robins was a quick-change artist. After emptying its pockets, he shed the coat. Then he whipped off his suit and wig—and was now wearing a dress and female wig. Costumed as a woman, he gave a recital on a prop violin. And pleased with his performance, he presented himself with a bouquet of flowers.

Finally, from his trunk he removed three bins; they were

---

* To hear that screech of delight, go to http://drama2014.furman.edu/BananaMan/index.html and play "Hear the Banana Man's haunting song!"

filled with the items he had produced. Robins transformed the trunk into a locomotive; connected the bins to it; quick-changed into the uniform of a railway conductor; and wheeled the train off stage. Upon returning for a bow, he wore a chestful of medals.

A. Robins deserved a medal, as an inventor as well as a performer. For he designed and built his own props. All of them—the oboe, the music stand, the stool, the watermelons, the bananas—were made of paper-mâché, cloth, or cardboard. And they were ingeniously designed to collapse and compress, then expand when needed. The article in *Mechanix Illustrated* describes the bananas:

> These bananas, typical of Robins' collapsible props, are made of carefully painted cloth covers stretched over springs which are fastened to six thin brass rods on a single base. Compressed, the 296 bananas can be folded into a space about twice the size of a cigar box. By mechanical releases they can be taken off in any number of bunches.

He simply touched its release spring, and a prop expanded as it left his pocket.

It took Robins two-and-a-half hours to load the coat for his ten-minute act. Fully loaded, it weighed 65 pounds. "When I come on stage," he said, "I feel heavy and tired. I'm suffering from the heat. Then I start to work. The faster and longer I work, the lighter I feel and the cooler I get. When I walk off, I'm feeling fine."

By the 1940s, however, the weight and heat of the coat had become too much for the aging clown. Moreover, vaudeville was in its final days. He retired from performing and moved with his wife to suburban New York. There he kept busy with a business he had started: the Tip Top Toy Company. In a basement workshop he designed and built wooden toys; the designs were then sold to manufacturers. Photographed in his workshop, Robins is bald, roly-poly, and impish-looking. He appears content with his new life as a toymaker.

But his stage persona did not join him in retirement. For

he had licensed his act to an entertainer named Sam Levine. Throughout the 1950s and 1960s, Levine performed on television as "A. Robins the Banana Man." He was a regular guest on the Captain Kangaroo show. Captain Kangaroo would introduce him; and Levine would waddle onto the set—wearing the original coat and wig, pulling the original trunk, and duplicating the original act. Anyone who remembers seeing the Banana Man, most likely saw Sam Levine.

Levine died in 1974. And the Banana Man paraphernalia—the coat, the collapsible bananas, and all the rest—came into the possession of Max Roth, who had been Levine's agent. These relics filled eight theatrical trunks. The trunks were eventually sold by Roth's widow, to a Brooklyn man who kept them in a storage locker. There they remained until 2003, when purchased by a fan from Tennessee.

It is unlikely that the act will ever be revived. But the Banana Man is still cackling and pulling things from his pockets—on YouTube. Here is a link to the only known footage of Robins performing. It is a shortened version of his act, with no bananas:

https://www.youtube.com/watch?v=KpVkRu0QkE8

And here is the entire act, complete with bananas, as performed by Sam Levine:

https://www.youtube.com/watch?v=yfJqLKM3dtw

Follow these links (or do a search on YouTube), and behold the unique spectacle that was the Banana Man.

Cardini

RICHARD PITCHFORD WAS BORN IN MUMBLES, A FISHing village in Wales, in 1895. He received little schooling; and at a young age, was apprenticed to a butcher. Yet he would become a magician—one whose stage persona was that of a tipsy aristocrat, and who was billed as "The Suave Deceiver." How did this come about?

His entry in *Vaudeville Old and New: An Encyclopedia of Variety Performers in America* describes Pitchford's metamorphosis:

> Although noted for his deft manipulations and comic pantomime rather than grand illusions, "The Suave Deceiver" was the master of one great transformation: that of changing himself from a Welsh lad from the factories into his stage depiction of a debonair, upper-class Britisher confounded by a profusion of cards, handkerchiefs, billiard balls and lit cigarettes. It was not a transformation quickly accomplished.

It had begun, in fact, when Pitchford was seven years old. He and his mother were living in Treharris, a mining town. She ran a boarding house for touring actors. One of the guests was a magician, who taught young Richard a few tricks, including the cut-and-restored rope. The boy was soon performing magic for his friends.

At the age of eight he was apprenticed to a butcher. But he found the work to be uncongenial; and after a year of it, ran away from home. In Cardiff he found work as a bellhop in a hotel. His education now began. A traveling salesman taught him how to stack a deck of cards. The manager of the billiard room tutored him in the game. And he learned —and diligently practiced—sleight-of-hand maneuvers, such as the front and back palming of a card.

When he was nineteen, World War I broke out; and Pitchford enlisted in the army. In the trenches he practiced with a deck of cards. In a hospital, after being wounded, he continued to practice. When the war ended, he returned to Cardiff; studied *The Art of Magic* by T. Nelson Downs; and purchased some props.

And he began his career as a magician. At theatres in Wales he found occasional work. Then, moving to London, he got a job at a department store—demonstrating tricks at the magic counter. Meanwhile, as "Professor Thomas," he gave lessons, He also performed on the street, passing the hat.

In 1923 Pitchford sailed to Australia, paying his passage by working as a steward on the ship. In Australia, as "Val Raymond," he performed in music halls. It was a standard act—tricks with cards, silks, doves, rabbits, boxes and other magical apparatus. But fate was about to intervene and propel him in a new direction.

A booking agent, for the Tivoli circuit, had invited him to audition. On the morning of the audition, Pitchford showed up at the theatre; but his trunks—with the paraphernalia for his act—failed to arrive. So he went to a pub, downed a whiskey, returned to the theatre, and took the stage. And for half-an-hour he improvised an act, using nothing but cards and cigarettes.

The agent was impressed by this act and hired him to perform it. But "Val Raymond"? He urged Pitchford to adopt a more distinctive name. They came up with "Cardini."

Never again would he need the contents of those trunks. For Cardini (as he called himself thereafter) had an act that was simple, innovative, and compelling. It was an immediate hit.

For three years he performed in Australia. Then he crossed the ocean and toured the U.S. So distinctive was his act that bookings were plentiful.

In Chicago he found himself in need of an assistant. And once again fate took a hand. The cashier at his hotel was a young, attractive woman named Swan Walker. Though lacking any experience, she was willing to venture on stage; and Cardini hired her. Before leaving Chicago, he also married her. They continued on the tour together, and would remain together for the next forty years.

By the time he reached New York, for an engagement at the Palace (*the* vaudeville theatre), Cardini had perfected his act. Originally, he had accompanied his sleight-of-hand maneuvers with a jocular patter. But the patter, he realized, was unnecessary and even detrimental. So he dropped it and became a pantomime—a performer whose every gesture was expressive. Accompanied by music, his moves now seemed choreographed. And his act—which would change little over the years that followed—had become a tour de force.

Of what did that act consist?

It began with a tipsy gentleman—Cardini—strolling onto the stage. After a night on the town he has returned to his hotel, in a state of mild intoxication. He wears evening clothes—top hat, tuxedo, cape, and gloves; carries a walking stick; and squints through a monocle. In the hotel lobby he hands his newspaper to a bellhop, played by Swan. And he begins a series of sleight-of-hand maneuvers that are both accomplished and comical.

Most magicians assume the role of a wizard with supernatural powers—a sorcerer who, with a wave of his wand, causes things to happen. Cardini's tipsy gentleman was different. "When I'm working out there," he told a journalist, "I try to convey the impression that I'm not doing any conjuring tricks. I think of myself as if I am drunk and surprised by what's going on."

Magical things happen *to* Cardini—he is their object, not their author; and they confound him. Cards appear in his hand. Befuddled, he throws them away—and more pop into his hand. The cards keep on appearing, as he litters the stage with them. Another magician would have taken credit for these materializations. Cardini, playing a drunk, is bewildered by them—though he does take an occasional bow.

He performs a similar routine with lit cigarettes. No sooner has he tossed one cigarette aside than another appears in his hand or mouth. His befuddlement grows. At one point he finds himself trying to smoke three cigarettes at once. And as he lurches about, a lit cigar appears in his hand, and then a pipe.

Cardini combined a mastery of sleight of hand with a comic persona. This combination brought him success—initially, on the vaudeville stage; then, with the decline of vaudeville, in nightclubs. Reviews of his act were invariably laudatory. The Camden *Evening Courier,* for example, had this to say:

> The reviewer has seen most of the card experts and illusionists in vaudeville, but Cardini is the peer of them all. His palming is uncanny. He grasps cards, balls, lighted cigarettes and other objects out of thin air. Above all, he has personality and showmanship.

Cardini would remain in the U.S. for the rest of his life. He and Swan resided in New York City, with their two children; but they were frequently on the road, traveling to engagements. In 1966 they retired.

Rare footage of their act may be viewed on YouTube. Go to http://www.youtube.com/watch?v=sVe7chIgn0w. (Or do a search for "Mago Victima—Cardini.") The video is nine minutes long; and when Cardini strolls off the stage—with a final bow—you may find yourself joining in the applause.

Dunninger

THE TERM *telepathy* WAS COINED BY F. W. H. MYERS, a founder of the Society for Psychical Research. In *Human Personality and Its Survival of Bodily Death* (1903), Myers defined telepathy as "the communication of impressions of any kind from one mind to another, independently of the recognized channels of sense." He believed that the phenomenon had far-reaching implications. "Among those implications," he declared, "none can be more momentous that the light thrown by this discovery upon man's intimate nature and possible survival of death."

Based on research conducted by the Society, Myers concluded that telepathy was real. Half a century later, millions of Americans would reach a similar conclusion. Their belief was inspired, however, by something less authoritative than research: a weekly television show. *The Dunninger Show* (or *The Amazing Dunninger,* as it was renamed after changing networks) was broadcast live, beginning in 1948. It featured an imposing figure known simply as Dunninger. An announcer introduced him to the studio audience as "the man who does the impossible, the world's foremost mentalist!" And Dunninger came on stage and performed feats of mindreading. So convincing were these feats that millions of viewers became believers in telepathy.

Who was Dunninger? And had he opened the eyes of those viewers to the reality of a psychic phenomenon—or had he hoodwinked them?

Born in 1892, Joseph Dunninger grew up on the Lower East Side of New York. His father, a tailor, was Catholic; his mother was Jewish. Both parents were immigrants from Germany. At an early age he was taken by an uncle to a magic show at the Academy of Music:

> I was between 6 and 8 years of age when I visited a theatre

> and witnessed the performance of Professor Kellar (at that time the world's greatest conjuror). Amazed and open-mouthed, I sat bewildered at the many marvelous things presented by this Master Wizard—the disappearing rabbits, the mysterious silks, the bowls of water produced out of thin air, and many other mystifying and equally impressive wonders. All were miraculous to me, and at once I felt within myself the desire to look into the pages of the secret volumes of magic, to learn how it was all done.

He was soon putting together tricks and performing for other boys. A single-minded desire—to become a magician—had gripped Joseph. As "Master Dunninger, the Child Wonder," he performed for a Masonic club and other groups. Photos of the child magician show him wearing a Little Lord Fauntleroy suit. During his teens he kept improving his act, and found occasional work at carnivals and dime museums. His social life consisted largely of hanging out with other magicians, in the back room of Martinka's magic shop.

Such were his skills as a performer—and as a self-promoter—that "Professor Dunninger," as he was calling himself, began to attract attention. When he was nineteen, his picture appeared on the cover of *The Sphinx,* a journal for magicians. But magic was still a sideline; to support himself he was working at a department store.

Then came a break. In 1914 he was hired by the Eden Musee, a wax museum and entertainment center on West Twenty-third Street. For more than a year he performed there daily. After that he was able to find work in vaudeville. On stage Dunninger looked the part of a magician—almost comically so. Tall and handsome, with shoulder-length hair, he wore a long Prince Albert coat and a white vest. His act consisted of standard routines—one of which was mind-reading.

For five years he eked out a living as a vaudevillian. Then came the turning point in his career. He acquired an agent—a savvy New Yorker named Florence King. Before seeking bookings for him, King did a complete makeover on Dunninger. She urged him to improve his diction. (His Lower East Side origins were evident in his speech.) She sent him to a barber—the long hair had to go. And she told him to get rid of the Prince Albert coat and to wear a plain suit. King insisted too that he drop the "Professor." Henceforth he was to perform simply as "Dunninger."

But the main change insisted upon by King involved the content of his act. He was told to scrap everything except the mindreading—*and to become a mentalist.* For therein, felt King, lay his greatest strength.

The agent knew her stuff. For the new Dunninger—"Dunninger the Amazing Mindreader"—was almost immediately a hit. During the 1920s his career soared. He landed a contract with the Keith-Orpheum circuit, and became a headliner at theatres around the country.

Reviewers were lavish in their praise of him:

> "Nothing like his performance has ever before been seen in vaudeville, and his feats in mindreading are simply unbelievable. His marvelous performance is astounding."—*Philadelphia Star*

> "Dunninger is the weirdest, most uncanny mystery ever presented before the American public."—*Boston American*

> "Dunninger at the Palace yesterday presented feats that were thoroughly mystifying.... Dunninger remains an interesting enigma."—*New York Times*

> "Never have I come in contact with such a dazzling, intriguing, and actually scientific mindreader, as the man Dunninger."—*Chicago Daily News*

Yet his rise was not without controversy. For Dunninger did not present himself as a magician. Rather, he claimed actually to be reading minds. No trickery was involved, he assured his audiences—just a rare ability that he possessed. "I read minds," he explained, "through the possession of extrasensory faculties, if you will—an extra sense, cultivated, sharpened, concentrated until the accidental manifestations familiar to everyone have, in me, matured to an unfailing technique of repetition."

This claim aroused the wrath of both scientists and magicians. The former were outraged by his insistence that his work was "scientific." No, they cried, it was fakery! Clearly, Dunninger was just another stage magician—a master of deception, who was falsely representing himself; and it was their duty to expose him. But in describing his powers, Dunninger was always careful to maintain a studied ambiguity. As Samuel Soal (a psychic researcher and author of *Preliminary Studies of a Vaudeville Telepathist*) says of mindreaders: "Instead of admitting that they are entertainers and disclaiming extra-sensory powers, they take refuge in non-committal phrases."

Meanwhile, his fellow magicians accused Dunninger of giving them a bad name. He was causing their profession to be associated with fake mediums, fortunetellers, and the like. A stage magician was a legitimate entertainer, they argued, whose feats were understood to be deceptions and were enjoyed as such. But Dunninger, in their view, had crossed a line and was engaged in fraud. His presentation of himself as a genuine "thought-reader" (a term he preferred to "mindreader," with its connotations of trickery) was deceitful and absurd. As one magician remarked: "Dunninger can't read the mind of a gnat and he knows it."

But Dunninger left it up to those in the audience to decide if he was genuine. And many believed that he was. For they were taken in by the scientific trappings of his act.

The act remained popular throughout the 1920s and 1930s. Dunninger drew large audiences to theatres. He also performed at private functions, entertaining at the homes of such notables as J. P. Morgan and Thomas Edison. ("Never have I witnessed anything as mystifying or seemingly impossible," said Edison.) Then, in 1943, he brought his mindreading, and other psychic abilities, to a new venue: radio. And his baritone voice, with its slight pseudo-British accent, would become familiar to millions.

Dunninger had experimented with radio twice before. In 1923 he had spoken into a microphone in a Long Island studio, and hypnotized a subject in the offices of *Science and Invention* (a magazine for which he wrote a column), ten miles away. Observing the subject were scientists and reporters, who verified that he had been hypnotized. And six years later Dunninger hosted *The Ghost Hour.* On it he sought to project his thoughts to listeners, who were told to relax, empty their minds, and be ready with pencil and paper. He also exposed fake mediums on the show. (They were giving genuine psychics like himself a bad name!) *The Ghost Hour* was short-lived. But in September 1943 *Dunninger the Master Mind* premiered on NBC. This time his commanding presence came through on radio; and the new show—sponsored initially by Kem-Tone paints, then by Rinso laundry soap—was a success. For three years it was broadcast weekly from a studio in New York, to a nationwide audience.

A 1946 press release (used to promote his personal appearances) describes the show:

DUNNINGER INTRODUCED TELEPATHY TO RADIO AND HAD LISTENERS AGOG

Even the radio editors who are always crying for something new under the sun gasped when they heard that Dunninger was bringing telepathy to the ether waves back on September 12, 1943. Even the most progressive souls smiled politely and shook their heads. It wasn't possible, they said. But the great Master Mind of Mental Mystery, who will give a personal demonstration of his remarkable ability at __________ on __________, accomplished the most marvelous feat ever conceived of in the history of radio. On that Sunday afternoon three years ago, he not only tuned in on thought waves broadcast to him from individuals in the radio studio audience, but he reached out telepathically over a distance of many miles and successfully interpreted the thoughts of persons he had never seen nor talked to....

During his many radio broadcasts, the mentalist has

> achieved such seemingly impossible results as conducting a "mental treasure hunt," opening a safe by telepathy, breaking a glass by concentration, describing the contents of a locked and sealed box, and many other unheard of feats.
>
> He has also projected his thoughts to others in the studio and has sent thought waves out over the radio, which a remarkable percentage of his listeners received and sent into the network by mail. He has also received messages from members of his listening audience miles away. All of his studio experiments were conducted under the watchful eyes of a committee of prominent individuals acting as guest judges, and these celebrities have attested to the authenticity of his experiments.

Prior to the broadcast, members of the studio audience were given slips of paper. They were told to write down a fact about themselves or a question. The slips were then sealed in envelopes. Dunninger circulated amongst the audience to assist in the sealing and collection of the slips.

The show began with Dunninger coming on stage and delivering a brief lecture. Then he sat down and instructed everyone to concentrate on what they had written on the slips. Clutching his head, he searched for "impressions." And he successfully read the minds of persons in the audience. Skeptics, of course, accused him of having palmed, and secretly read, their slips.

The high point of the radio show was the Brain Buster test. Each week Dunninger was subjected to a test of his psychic abilities. These stunts were the creation of a former mentalist named David Lustig, whom Dunninger had hired as an idea man. Once a week Lustig came up with a new Brain Buster—so-called, it was explained, for the extreme mental exertion the tests required of Dunninger. He was challenged, for example, to read the mind of the pilot of an airplane, who was in touch with the studio via radio. He was challenged to read the mind of a person on the Parachute Jump at Coney Island. And he was challenged to open a safe at the National Jewelry Exchange—by reading the minds of two guards, each of whom knew half of the

combination. In each case he was successful.

In 1948 the show made the transition to television; and the Brain Busters became even more impressive. In one of them, Dunninger induced the postmaster of New York City to participate. An account of the test appeared in *Hugard's Magic Monthly* for August 1953:

> One of his best recent stunts was a twist on his familiar sealed prophecy test. In this one he wrote in advance the name and address of an envelope later to be selected, also the sender's name and address and the postmark. He sealed the cardboard in an envelope and passed it to three newsmen. *If you didn't recognize Bob Dunn, the method may have puzzled you.* [In addition to being a newsman, Dunn was an amateur magician—and probably a friend of Dunninger's.] On the screen the postmaster of the N. Y. Post Office was seen by a conveyor belt. Sacks of mail went past. He selected one. Opened it, spilled out the letters. Then he

> chose one. The camera took a closeup. *The three newsmen made notes of what was written on it, then Dunninger's prediction was opened. Success!* The information was the same!

At the height of his professional success, however, Dunninger suffered a personal setback. For years he had been maintaining two residences in New York. In one of them he lived with his mother. In the other he kept a mistress: a former dancer named Chrystal Spencer. He had met Spencer —"the South Seas Island dancer and recent sensation of Broadway," as she was billed—in 1922. Joining his show as an assistant, she became his companion as well. But twenty years later, Dunninger's ardor had cooled; and he was covertly seeing another woman. After a tumultuous scene—both women had shown up at his mother's home one night and confronted him—Spencer took Dunninger to court. Claiming to be his common-law wife, she demanded—and was granted—alimony.*

What sort of man was Dunninger? His public persona was intimidating. Here was someone who could stare at you and read your mind! William Rauscher, author of *The Mind Readers: Masters of Deception* (2002), describes him as "dominant, commanding, and charismatic." Dunninger the mentalist was a kind of hypnotist—an entertainer who

---

* In his will Dunninger left ten dollars to Spencer. He declared that she had never been his wife, common-law or otherwise, and that the findings of the court had been based upon "her false and perjured testimony."

For a more sympathetic view of her, visit the Chrystal Dunninger Museum. The museum "is located in San Jose, California, in a dresser drawer," according to its curator, and consists of scrapbooks and other articles acquired from Chrystal's family. But it may be visited on-line, at http://www.cindythings.com/chrystalhome.htm. The on-line version is "a one-of-a-kind biographical tour of the world's only historical collection of photographs and personal belongings of Chrystal Dunninger, celebrated beauty, professional dancer, magician, and world traveler—and wife of the greatest mentalist who ever lived, Joseph Dunninger."

could hold an audience spellbound by the force of his personality. But what of Dunninger the man? No one seems to have really known him—not even Chrystal Spencer, she admitted, despite twenty years together. He was as mysterious as his supposed powers—an enigma even to those closest to him.

In *It Takes All Kinds* (1952), a book about eccentrics, Maurice Zolotow has a chapter on Dunninger. He deems him to be "one of the great showmen of our time." But Zolotow notes the divide between the public figure and the private individual. "On the surface, he presents a picture of suavity, self-assurance, serenity." Beneath the surface, however, ran a darker current:

> That Dunninger's astounding success in show business has brought him any inner serenity is doubtful. There is a high price that one pays for carrying out a power operation as complicated and basically hostile to other people as Dunninger's pattern of setting himself up as the world's greatest mental telepathist. The cost is a human cost. It is loneliness, a daily life in which one is shut up alone with one's secrets, not daring to share thoughts or feelings with anyone, lest one's secrets leak out and be exposed. It is a life of constant hazards and threats. But for Dunninger no other way seems possible.

That loneliness was eased around the time of his television debut, when he married Billie Joa, a former dancer. They had met in the lobby of Bloomingdale's, when Billie dropped some packages and Dunninger helped her to pick them up. They would remain together until his death a quarter-century later.

Dunninger continued to perform until 1973, when ill health forced him into retirement. He retreated to their home in New Jersey and became reclusive, rarely leaving the house or receiving visitors. Billie took care of him.

William Rauscher paid him a visit there. "A dog barked incessantly," he recalls in *The Mind Readers*. "His study was a mishmash of books, papers, and Oriental artifacts. He looked unkempt.... The entire house was in disarray." Yet despite his frailty, says Rauscher, he had retained his aura of command.

But that aura was no longer needed. For Dunninger—who had once gazed imperiously at audiences in packed theatres and read their minds—had no one's thoughts left to read now save his own and Billie's.

Leon Mandrake

THE COMIC STRIP *Mandrake the Magician,* BY LEE FALK and Phil Davis, first appeared in 1934, and is still being published. Clad in top hat, tuxedo, and cape, Mandrake battles criminals, mad scientists, aliens, and other sociopaths. His chief weapon is the power of hypnosis. Gesturing hypnotically, he creates illusions so realistic as to frighten or befuddle his foes.*

He is aided in this crusade by a sidekick, a girlfriend, and a father in Tibet. The sidekick is Lothar, an African prince who is physically powerful and wears a fez. (Prior to a makeover in the sixties, he also wore a leopard skin, spoke Pidgin English, and addressed Mandrake as "Master.") The girlfriend (they finally married in 1997) is Princess Narda, from the kingdom of Cockaigne. And the father is Theron, head of the College of Magic in Tibet and guardian of the Crystal Cube.†

As for his foes, they include the Cobra, a scientist who keeps trying to steal the Crystal Cube; Octon, the head of a vast crime syndicate; and Ekardnam (*mandrake* spelled backwards), his evil twin, who dwells on the other side of the mirror. (Alice beware!) When not battling these malefactors, Mandrake relaxes in a palatial residence called Xanadu.**

Xanadu is located on a mountaintop; and with its chef,

---

* According to Lee Falk, Mandrake's look—top hat, tuxedo, cape, and pencil-thin mustache—was inspired by that of Cardini.

† It is possible that Theron was actually his stepfather, and that Mandrake's father was an itinerant magician known as Grando the Great. Conflicting accounts are given in the strip.

** *Mad* once published a parody of the strip, called "Manduck the Magician." Manduck lives in the county dump. But he has hypnotized himself into thinking that he resides in a fancy house.

swimming pool, and other amenities, is a haven for the hard-working crime fighter. It would have made a welcome retreat too for his namesake—the flesh-and-blood magician who called himself Leon Mandrake; who dressed like the comic-strip character; and who bedazzled audiences with his illusions.

Leon Giglio was born in 1911, the son of vaudevillians, and grew up in New Westminster, British Columbia. When he was eight, his aunt gave him a Mysto Magic set; and the boy was hooked. At the age of eleven he adopted a stage name—"the Wiz"—and appeared on the stage of the Edison, the local vaudeville theatre. At fourteen he performed in a carnival; two years later he was touring with the Ralph Richards magic show. And by the 1930s Leon the Ventriloquist, as he was calling himself, had his own show, and was making a living as a magician.

Opinions differ as to which Mandrake—the comic-strip character or Leon—was the first to bear the name. Some claim that Leon was first, and that the creator of *Mandrake the Magician* borrowed the name from him. Leon's son believes that the two arrived at the name independently. But according to an authority on the comic strip, Leon did not perform as Mandrake until five years after the strip first appeared.

That authority is a Norwegian who calls himself the Clay Camel, after one of Mandrake's foes. His Web site is a treasure trove of information about the fictional Mandrake. And it has this to say about Leon:

> There has been a real life Canadian born stage magician who use the name Mandrake the Magician. From 1939 until 1946 his wife and female assistant's stage name was "Narda" and his main male assistant's name was "Lothar." He toured extensively in the U.S. with his full evening show, with great success.
>
> In Chicago 1947 he met and married Velvet. Under the stage name "Leon Mandrake and Company," they did theatre shows and performed in the lavish night clubs of the 1940s and 1950s. While on tour, Leon met Phil Davis [the

> artist of the comic strip] in St. Louis, they became fast friends and corresponded for years.
>
> It is clear that Lee Falk [the creator of the strip] first use the name "Mandrake the Magician" because in the late 30s Leon Mandrake was known under the stage name "Leon the Ventriloquist"...
>
> It seems that Leon Mandrake had read the Mandrake daily strip "Mandrake in Love" [appearing from December 9, 1938 to March 12, 1939] and got inspired to make a stage show with Mandrake the Magician, Narda and Lothar.

So Leon seems to have appropriated the name and persona of the comic-strip character, and to have done so with the acquiescence of the artist. In any case, he would change his name legally to Mandrake. And the four children born to him and Velvet, his second wife, would bear that name.

Leon performed with Velvet (who had previously been one of Blackstone's showgirls) from 1947 onwards. Nightclubs were replacing theatres as the main venue for magic; and he successfully transitioned, while still doing an occasional stage show. His act included hypnotism, mindreading, escapes, levitation, and fire-eating. His featured trick was the Dancing Handkerchief.*

In the mid 1950s Leon's career took a curious turn. During the vaudeville era there had been a popular magician who billed himself as Alexander the Seer, wore a turban and robe, and specialized in mindreading. Towards the end of his life, he sold his entire show; and Leon acquired it—props, costumes, posters, secrets, and the rights to the name "Alexander." (It was registered with the National Vaudeville Association.) Donning the swami outfit and calling himself Alexander, Leon performed in nightclubs as a mentalist. So closely did he resemble the original Alexander that he was able to use the old posters for publicity. He also had a television show, called *Alexander the Great.* At the

* The Dancing Handkerchief, also known as Spirit in a Bottle, may be viewed at http://www.youtube.com/watch?v=mT-0gnyik4Q or found by searching for "Mandrake Dancing Handkerchief."

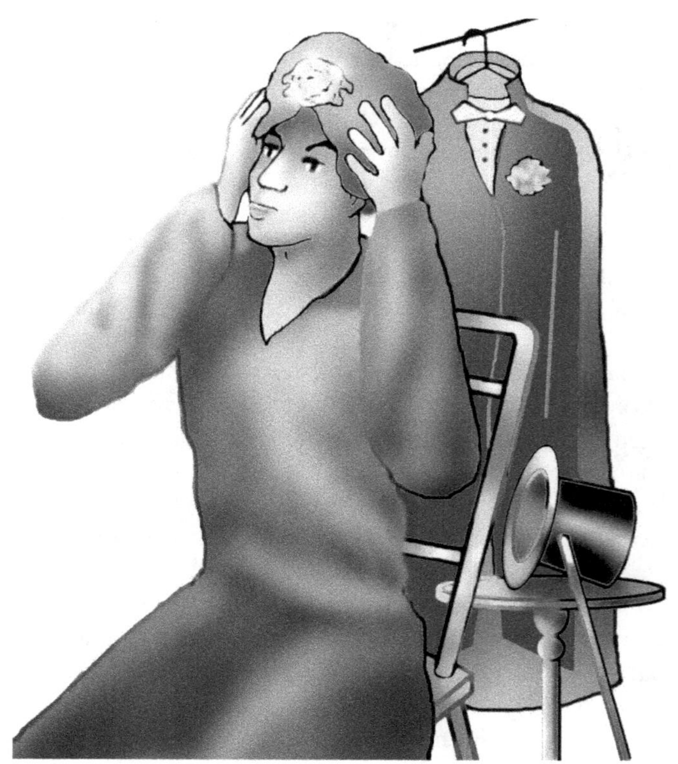

same time, he was still performing as Mandrake.*

* Occasionally, a nightclub would hire him to perform as both magicians: one night he was Mandrake; another night, Alexander. It is tempting to compare this duality with that of the comic-strip Mandrake and his evil twin, or with that of Dr. Jekyll and Mr. Hyde. For Leon—one of the most genial and well-regarded of magicians—was impersonating one of the most notorious. A mind-reader on stage, the original Alexander had also taken in money as a New Thought guru; operated as a fraudulent medium; and marketed Ouija boards and crystal balls. The latter came with a pamphlet titled "Crystal Gazing: Lessons and Instructions." He was married six times; had been prosecuted for extortion; and was rumored to have murdered a man. "Those who have researched Alexander," writes William Rauscher in *The Mind Readers: Masters of Deception,* "conclude that he was the ultimate cheat, crook, scoundrel, and a sinister, ruthless, and immoral man."

But after a few years of this dual identity, Leon gave it up. As Mandrake he continued to perform throughout the U.S. and Canada. And in 1967 he did a tour of the Orient, with shows in Japan, Hong Kong, Taiwan, and the Philippines.

Thereafter, he appeared mostly at trade shows, state fairs, and colleges—magic acts having gone out of style at nightclubs. Finally, after sixty years as a magician, he retired to his home in Surrey, British Columbia. There he lived until his death in 1993.

A memorial was held at the Edison, where—as the Wiz—he had begun his career at the age of eleven. The old vaudeville house was now a venue for exotic dancers. Their photos were taken down for the memorial.

Dantini the Magnificent

For fifteen years Dantini the Magnificent performed at the Peabody Book Shop and Beer Stube. A Baltimore landmark, the Book Shop had opened in 1927; the Beer Stube was added six years later. By the time of Dantini, however, no one came to buy books. The Book Shop was moribund, its few remaining books gathering dust. It served simply as the entryway to the Beer Stube. One passed through it to get to the drinking establishment in the back.

The Peabody Book Shop was once a major resource for Baltimoreans. Founded by Siegfried Weisberger, an Austrian immigrant, the shop was a cornucopia of second-hand books—tens of thousands of volumes. Weisberger was a booklover who enjoyed conversing with his customers; and when Prohibition ended, he converted the garage behind his shop into a beer room—a gathering place for the bookish. "Beer and books go together," he told a reporter.

But in 1954, Weisberger retired in disgust. It was indeed the Age of the Boob, he lamented, echoing the sentiments of his friend H. L. Mencken. "The people don't want books and ideals and culture. They only want dollars." He sold his entire stock of books to Gimbels in New York, and retired to his farm.

Yet the Peabody survived, under a new owner who transformed the beer room into a popular destination. Rose Smith ran the business for the next thirty years, while living in an apartment upstairs. Upon her death the Peabody closed. And for a decade the building sat vacant, with its sign, facade, and window display intact—as if the beer room were still open, for a ghostly clientele. Then the building was condemned, as structurally unsound, and demolished.

The Beer Stube had the feel of a colonial tavern. There

was a fireplace; and in the winter a fire warmed those sitting and carousing at the oaken tables. The room was smoke-filled and dimly lit. The light came from a wrought-iron chandelier, suspended from a beam of the vaulted ceiling. The clientele was a lively mix that included college students, musicians (from the nearby Peabody School of Music), artists, and tourists. They rubbed shoulders at the communal tables—tables into which generations of drinkers had carved their initials. The food accompanying the drinks was mediocre—"the worst food in the city," according to a review. But one came to the Peabody for its atmosphere. (That is to say, for its ambience—the actual atmosphere was thick with cigarette smoke.) And one came for the conviviality: spontaneous sing-alongs were a frequent occurrence. There was also entertainment: a pianist, a violinist, and a nightly magic show. The magic show featured Dantini the Magnificent.

Dantini was the resident magician at the Peabody. His show was eleven minutes long. It began at ten o'clock (with an additional show at midnight on weekends), and never varied. Wearing an Oriental cap, a rumpled black suit, and sneakers, Dantini performed in front of the piano. His long white beard gleamed in the light from the chandelier. "Good evening, ladies and gentlemen," he began. "I will try to entertain you with a few little magic tricks."

With slowed but practiced hands, Dantini did a card trick; vanished a lit cigarette; performed the Miser's Dream (coin after coin plucked from nowhere); manipulated a golf ball; pulled a scarf through the neck of a volunteer; and concluded with the Chinese Linking Rings. His patter during these tricks was the same every night—almost word for word. (Invariably, for example, the scarf trick had been "learned from the great Houdini himself.") His manner was low-key. And his expression was woeful. He seemed to have acquired, during his years of performing, a melancholy disposition.

When the show was over, there was a round of polite applause; and Dantini passed the hat for tips. (Actually, he

passed around the lower section of a dove pan—a utensil normally used for materializing doves.) Then he either chatted with patrons or else retreated to a dim corner to eat.

The show was mildly entertaining, though no more so than that of a competent amateur. And indeed, this "old geezer" (as a newspaper described him), with his unexceptional tricks, must have seemed like an amateur to the Peabody drinkers—among whom was an occasional heckler. They could not have known that Dantini was a seasoned performer—someone who had spent a lifetime as a magician, and who in his twilight years had found a berth at the Peabody.

He had begun his career at an early age. Vincent Cierkes—the future Dantini—was born in Baltimore, in 1906, and raised there, the son of Polish immigrants. But at fifteen he ran away from home. Hopping a freight train to Pittsburgh,

Vincent found work in vaudeville, doing magic tricks. He developed an act and took it to shows in other cities. And he spent his summers in a sideshow at Coney Island, performing as "Doctor Zangar, Jr." Eventually he adopted "Dantini" as his stage name.

Dantini performed in a variety of venues: circuses, carnivals, vaudeville theatres, nightclubs. He traveled throughout the eastern states, from job to job. Finally, however, he returned to Baltimore and settled there. In Baltimore he assisted Rajah Raboid, a local mindreader; performed briefly as a mindreader himself; and did magic tricks at a burlesque theatre, in between the strip acts. During the 1950s, he worked mainly in spook shows.

Spook shows were live events that preceded the midnight showings of horror movies. One or more magicians performed on the stage. Then the lights went out; eerie music filled the theatre; and special effects—ghosts projected onto cheesecloth, skeletons dangling on wires, and such—elicited screams from the audience.

In Baltimore spook shows were held at the old movie palaces—the Broadway, the Grand, the Hippodrome. A handbill for one show, in which Dantini appeared, describes what awaited the fearless: "Extraordinary Attraction! Do spirits return? Laffs, thrills, chills. Zombies' screams. Graveyard revue; vampires, spirit science, dancing skeleton, floating ghost girl."

But Dantini moved on. "I gave up the spook shows," he explained, "because they're kind of tough and dangerous to do. When the lights go out, anything can happen from the audience. They would throw something during the dark seance. I was always afraid of those spook shows."

When the Peabody hired him, in 1963, Dantini was living in Fells Point. This was the neighborhood in which he had grown up—the oldest section of Baltimore, adjacent to the harbor. His home was a dilapidated rowhouse, which he owned and could barely afford to maintain. (He saved money by going without heat in the winter.) The place had a minimum of furniture. But it was filled with memorabilia

—three floors of conjuring clutter. There were magic books, broken equipment, playbills, newspaper clippings, photographs, posters for spook shows, a rubber skull, mummy cases, a pair of leg irons that Houdini had used. Dantini lived alone with his memorabilia and memories. Yet he was not totally without companionship. In the morning, he would open a window and feed the pigeons that came fluttering in.

Dantini the Magnificent became a familiar figure in Baltimore—one of its prime eccentrics. He was often seen shuffling about town, dressed in a shabby coat, floppy hat, and battered sneakers. He pasted fliers for his show onto phone booths, and handed them out on buses. With his unkempt beard and scruffy garb, he might have been mistaken for a homeless man. Yet he had a home, a profession, and a modest income. What he lacked was an official identity. Dantini had no social security number, paid no income tax, had no bank account. (He kept his assets in cash, taped to the bottom of his bathtub.)

For years Dantini had dreamt of mounting a full stage show, and even had some props built for it. Alas, he never fulfilled this ambition. His nightly show at the Peabody remained his sole employment as a magician. But toward the end of his life, he did venture into a new area of the arts: filmmaking.

Financing it with his savings (withdrawn from beneath the tub), he produced, directed, starred in, and premiered a film called *Our Baltimore*. It was a documentary—"a nonprofit venture to promote Baltimore worldwide"—in which Dantini tours the city on foot. He visits its landmarks, such as the Shot Tower and Poe's grave. And he meets with local luminaries, including William Donald Schaefer (the mayor of Baltimore and a fellow eccentric) and Blaze Starr (the striptease artist). For the "world premiere" of the film he rented the 13,000-seat Civic Center. The event included live performances by local magicians and other entertainers. A midget friend of Dantini's served as emcee. Tickets were sold at the door. But fewer than a hundred people showed up to see the film—a fiasco that left Dantini broke.

He continued to perform at the Peabody. But on March 9, 1979, the curtain fell forever on Dantini's act. It was a Friday night; and the beer room was crowded and boisterous. The pianist and violinist were playing.

Dantini was waiting to go on for his midnight show. Beside him stood Rose the owner. All at once, he began "acting strangely," she would tell a reporter. He was concerned that the musicians were encroaching on his performance time. "Dantini knew the two men who were performing, but he suddenly turned to me and said, 'It's my time to go on. I must go on now.' So I told him to go up and start jingling his rings and rattling around so that the others would get the message. He did just that and then did his regular magic act."

When he had finished, Dantini shuffled back and rejoined her. He was not feeling well, he said. "Then he sat down on a chair in the gallery between the bookstore and the beer stube. He suddenly toppled off the chair.... He lost consciousness."

An ambulance was called; and Dantini was taken to the hospital. There, after five days in a coma, he died. That midnight show had been his swan song. Somehow he had known that the hour had come for his final performance.*

A filmmaker named Buchman had played piano at the Peabody; had gotten to know Dantini; and had made a short film about him. He had this to say in remembrance of the magician:

> Dantini was a fascinating man, overwhelmingly tragic and overwhelmingly human, a perfect subject for a film. He possessed more energy, dignity, self-assurance and professionalism than many so-called "star" performers have today.
>
> Dantini's act at the Peabody Bookshop, where he performed regularly for the past several years, was a much-

* According to legend, swans are mute until the moment of their death—at which time they sing a song and expire.

condensed version of his original vaudeville routine, reduced to including only small sleight-of-hand tricks. But he never openly admitted the "big time" passed him by. He approached each performance as if he were playing the old Palace Theater in New York, and even when the Peabody drinkers heckled him, he knew he was the star, and he made his exits triumphant....

He never gave up. Despite his age, despite the fact that people mocked him and laughed at him, he refused to quit.

Myrus the Mentalist

IN OCTOBER OF 1959, MYRUS THE MENTALIST WAS INTERviewed by two reporters from the *Wiley Wigwam.* The *Wigwam* was the school newspaper of the Frank L. Wiley Junior High School, located in a suburb of Cleveland. And the fifteen-year-old journalists—Sue Katzel and Steve Solomon (the illustrator of this book)—had arrived at his suite in the Fenway Hall Hotel, "expecting," they would write, "a creaking door to open and a turbaned telepathist to invite them in."

But the man who opened the door was, to their relief, "not a swami with piercing eyes." Rather, the "famous mentalist" had a look in his eye that was more bemused than piercing. No turban covered his graying hair. And he was wearing a suit rather than a robe. Myrus welcomed them, led them inside, and answered their questions.

Then he gave a demonstration of his powers. Handing them slips of paper, he instructed his visitors to write down the names of their mothers. He took the folded slips and held them to his forehead. Think of those names, said Myrus. And to the reporters' astonishment, he told them the names of their mothers!

They departed with a glossy photo of Myrus, a memorable experience, and a story for the *Wigwam.**

The article that appeared in the paper was headlined MYRUS CONVINCES WIGWAM SKEPTICS. It was accompanied by the photo, in which Myrus is seen gazing into a mirror—

* My brother Steve tells me that, during the interview, he sought to suppress any skeptical thoughts; for he was worried that Myrus would read his mind and be offended by his skepticism. And Sue Katzel, now a retired psychotherapist, recalls being affected by the personality of the mentalist. He seemed so serious a person, she says—so forceful a presence.

as if reading his own mind. And it described how the mentalist had discovered his ability while still in elementary school. He had found himself anticipating what the teacher was about to write on the blackboard. In high school and college, he had experimented further with telepathy. Finally, he had embarked upon a career as a nightclub performer. As to the nature of his ability, "he does not know how or why the strange power of mental telepathy comes to him, and he has no control over it." But that power was real, the article concluded. "Myrus is an ordinary fellow with an extra-ordinary power beyond the realm of understanding."

At the time of the interview, Myrus was well-known locally. He had a weekly television show in Cleveland, broadcast live from the studios of WJW-TV. For half-an-hour he performed his mindreading act before a studio audience—the same act he had been performing, for nearly three decades, in nightclubs around the country.

Before the show, members of the studio audience were given blank cards and envelopes. They were told to write a question on the card; fold it so as to hide the question; seal it in the envelope; and initial the envelope. The envelopes were then collected and deposited in a glass-sided hopper. And the show began.

Myrus came on stage, dressed in a suit and tie. He talked about his ability to receive mental impressions. Then he drew an envelope from the hopper, read aloud the initials, and asked that person to rise and think of the question.

The mentalist held the envelope to his forehead. It was to serve, he explained, as a kind of touchstone to the thought. He furrowed his brow, straining to read the mind of the person who was standing. And he began to answer the question—in general terms at first, then more specifically as the impressions came into focus.

Finally, he opened the envelope and read its contents aloud. And the audience applauded; for indeed, he had answered the question. Myrus drew more envelopes from the hopper. Each time he called out the initials and instructed that person to rise. And one after another, he succeeded in reading their minds. Or so it seemed. For each time he would open the envelope and confirm his success.

Who was this man with the amazing ability? Not much is known about Myrus. His real name was Harry Carp; he was Jewish; and he was originally from Chicago. He worked in nightclubs, with his wife Melba serving as his assistant. In ads he was billed as "the Wizard of Mental Telepathy," or as "the Man with the X-Ray Eyes." And he was a popular attraction. In 1944, for example, he completed a forty-week engagement in New York, at the Cotillion Room of the Pierre Hotel. From there Myrus traveled to Palm Beach, where he was a featured performer at the Jardin Royal. (According to the *Palm Beach Post,* the act proved to be "a great drawing card.") He and Melba were often on the road, staying at hotels favored by performers. His television show in Cleveland was the closing chapter in a long and successful career. When the show ended in the early sixties, the couple moved permanently to their winter home in Florida.

Were his powers genuine? Myrus claimed that they were; and many believed him. How else could he have known what people were thinking? But mentalism is a branch of conjuring; and the "Q&A mindreading act" (as it is known in the profession) has long been performed by magicians. They could reveal exactly how Myrus was able to read minds.

For Myrus was a magician rather than a psychic. Yet he never let on that trickery was involved. He identified himself as an entertainer with psychic powers. And he never associated with other magicians—never visited the local magic shop to chat with his brethren. Thus was he able to preserve his mystique as the Wizard of Mental Telepathy.

•

Dorothy Fuldheim was a popular talk-show host in Cleveland, who from time to time had Myrus on as a guest. She lent him credibility, by seeming to believe in his powers. But did she really? Or was Fuldheim mischievously pretending to believe, and joining in the fun?

In any case, Myrus was a well-known figure in Cleveland—and the subject of debate. According to a report in the *Plain Dealer,* his act "has aroused much discussion. Some are convinced that the man can read your mind while others obstinately insist that his mental feats are practiced by all the magical fraternity."

Among the doubters was Professor Raleigh M. Drake, head of the Psychology Department at Kent State University. Myrus had met with the professor, who was eager to subject him to a series of tests. But in a letter to the *Plain*

Dealer, Drake declared that Myrus had refused to take the tests and "had no telepathic abilities whatsoever." Myrus replied to the letter as follows:

> Thank you for the opportunity afforded me to answer the somewhat inaccurate and ill-tempered letter concerning me sent to you by Prof. Drake of Kent State University.
>
> I don't particularly mind if Professor Drake wants to take pot shots at me from his academic ivory tower and I refuse to enter a name-calling contest with a man as obviously prejudiced in his attitude toward my professional performances.
>
> I do, however, resent some of Professor Drake's statements which do not reflect the truth.
>
> I have never claimed the powers of extra-sensory perception to the extent that he insists I have. I consistently and openly maintain that the impressions of other persons' thoughts are no more than compulsive impressions to me and I interpret them as such. It is unimportant to me whether or not they meet Professor Drake's qualifications.
>
> All I know is that since I went on television in February, 1954, the program, "What's On Your Mind," has been satisfactorily interesting and intriguing as entertainment to thousands of viewers. I have never claimed any more pretentious ambitions for the program, or my work....
>
> After traveling to Kent State last May 10 at Professor Drake's invitation, I encountered an atmosphere of such obvious belligerence and antagonism as a "guest" of the psychology department that I could see no useful purpose being served by a subsequent meeting.
>
> Two of the experiments that Professor Drake stressed were tests of telepathy had absolutely no bearing on the subject. One was to pick from lettered cubes placed face down, the name of a book (in mental telepathy one establishes contact with another human being—not inanimate objects such as cubes). Professor Drake asked me to read the written sentence that was in the pocket of a Kent professor at that moment in a plane on his way to New York. This has no bearing on telepathy as the person must be in contact with me either in the same room or by telephone. In this case there was no possible way of human contact.

> Incidentally, I demonstrated successfully, the same type of experiments I conduct on television, with Professor Drake's colleagues at Kent State. Professor Drake insisted they were not thought transference, but when he was asked what they were, that is when Professor Drake ducked.
>
> My business is entertaining people. Professor Drake's business is teaching psychology. I suggest we both stick to our business, as name-calling is foreign to my nature and unbecoming to Professor Drake's position.

A dignified response to an "inaccurate and ill-tempered" skeptic!

John Calvert

SINCE ANCIENT TIMES, MEN HAVE SOUGHT THE SECRET of longevity. They have tried to concoct the Elixir of Life, or to locate the Fountain of Youth. According to Herodotus, the Fountain of Youth was to be found in Africa:

> The Ichthyophagi [Fish-Eaters], in their turn, questioned the prince concerning the duration of life in Ethiopia, and the kind of food there in use: they were told that the majority of the people lived to the age of one hundred and twenty years, but that some exceeded even that period; that their meat was baked flesh, their drink milk. When the spies expressed astonishment at the length of life in Ethiopia, they were conducted to a certain fountain, in which having bathed, they became shining as if anointed with oil, and diffused from their bodies the perfume of violets.... If their representation of this water was true, the constant use of it may probably explain the extreme length of life which the Ethiopians attain.

Or was it elsewhere? Alexander the Great thought the Fountain of Youth was in India. Ponce de Leon looked for it while exploring Florida. A medieval legend located it "to the east," in the kingdom of Prester John. And a Polynesian legend placed it in Hawaii.

Whatever its location, magician John Calvert seems to have found it and drunk of its waters. For Calvert—who first performed on a stage in 1929—was still performing in 2013. He was 102 years old.

Calvert was born in 1911 in New Trenton, a small town in Indiana. When he was eight, his father took him to Cincinnati, to see the Howard Thurston show. Inspired by what he saw, the boy taught himself magic. And by the time he was eighteen, Calvert had put together a show. Accompanied by an assistant and Gyp the Wonder Dog, he traveled the back roads of Kentucky, performing in theatres and town halls.

As the show became more elaborate, his car was no longer adequate for transporting the props. So he began using a trailer, then a small truck. Increasingly, Calvert was in demand as a performer. Acquiring a tractor-trailer, he hauled his show from engagement to engagement. And by the mid 1940s he was transporting it—the props, sets, and cast members—in a DC-3. The plane had JOHN CALVERT painted on its side, and was piloted by the magician himself. The show had become an extravaganza, advertised as having "lavish sets" and "a bevy of beauties."

Meanwhile, he had begun a second career, as a movie actor. His first role was in *Honky Tonk,* as a stand-in for Clark Gable's hands. Gable was playing a magician; and when the magician's hands were seen in close-up—doing

card tricks—they were Calvert's. His hands proved to be his "foot in the door." Between 1940 and 1957, Calvert acted in more than forty films, and directed several others. His earliest parts were as magicians and as villains in Westerns. Later he starred (the third actor to do so) in the series of films about the Falcon, a debonair detective. Tall, handsome, and debonair himself, John Calvert was perfectly cast as the Falcon.

Calvert made his home in Hollywood, and was kept busy as an actor. Yet he continued to perform as a magician. His contract with Columbia Pictures gave him paid leave for three months each year. During that time he was on the road, or in the air, with his magic show. But in 1957—after producing, writing, directing, and starring in *Dark Venture,* shot on location in Africa—he decided to leave movies and devote himself entirely to magic.*

In the years that followed, Calvert made repeated tours of the Far East with his company. The show—props, sets, and that bevy of beauties—was traveling by sea now, in his private yacht. He was the last magician to conduct "world tours in the grand manner," as he described them. His illusions, which included a levitation and a vanishing elephant, were not original; but he presented them with skill and showmanship. And he performed to music, which he believed essential for engaging an audience. The show played to sold-out houses in Japan, Taiwan, the Philippines, Malaysia, and Singapore—countries in which John Calvert the Magician was a popular, and exotic, attraction.

Calvert married three times. Each wife was acquired during a different phase of his career. During his debut as a magician, at a theatre in Bowling Green, Kentucky, he

---

* Thirty-five years later he reissued *Dark Venture* as *Curse of the Elephants' Graveyard.* In an added prologue and epilogue, the main characters—played by Calvert and Ann Cornell, now in their eighties—reminisce about their journey to the Elephants' Graveyard.

Perhaps it was during his travels in Africa that Calvert did in fact locate—and drink from—the Fountain of Youth.

charmed the twenty-year-old ticket-seller. They wound up getting married and having a daughter; but the marriage did not last. Then, at the height of his film career, Calvert married actress Ann Cornell, who became his assistant in the magic show. The marriage lasted fourteen years. Finally, during his second tour of the Far East, a nineteen-year-old Malaysian actress joined his bevy of beauties. "Tammy," as he dubbed her, soon became his assistant, and then his wife. Fifty years later, they were still married.

And they were still performing together—touring with a stage show called Magicarama. In 2008 John Calvert came full circle. Magicarama played for a week at the Capitol Theatre in Bowling Green—the very theatre at which, eighty years before, he had launched his career and charmed the ticket-seller. Assisted by Tammy, he presented "a full two hour dynamic evening of magic and illusion," as it was advertised. The featured illusion was The Flying Organ, in which he levitated Tammy and a pipe organ.

Magicarama received good reviews. One of them noted that Tammy—nearly seventy-years-old now—seemed as ageless as her husband:

> Tammy does a wonderful job of misdirecting the action throughout the watch routine. You can see that Tammy is as skilled at her job as John is at his. Not to mention that Tammy looks absolutely great! John did pass along his secrets to longitivity [sic] including good clean living and thinking like a young man.

But finally, Calvert lowered the curtain for the last time on Magicarama, and became semi-retired. He and Tammy took up residence in Bowling Green, in order to be near his daughter by the ticket-seller. Yet he still traveled about, lecturing and performing at magic clubs and conventions.

In 2011—the year of his hundredth birthday—Calvert published a short book, titled *How to Live to Be a Hundred* (SPS Publications). In it he makes no mention of the Fountain of Youth. But he does offer this advice: "Do your exercises, don't be a television addict, keep moving, watch your diet, eat the right food, and drink plenty of liquids."

But the inevitable at last caught up with him. John Calvert died on September 27, 2013, in California, with Tammy at his side. He was 102 years old. Just a week before, he had given the performance that turned out to be his last.

Professor Solomon

My first venture into show business was as Mr. Sneakers, the mascot of a shoe company. The company manufactured a shoe whose brand name was Mr. Sneakers. Its logo was a clown; and an actor was to have portrayed the clown at a Los Angeles trade fair. But the actor had fallen ill; and a substitute had been hired to take his place. That substitute—a graduate student in film studies at U.C.L.A.—was me.

On a Saturday morning I arrived at the hotel where the trade fair—an annual event that brought together manufacturers and retailers—was being held. I located the Mr. Sneakers booth and introduced myself. (I had been hired by phone.) One of the salesmen handed me my costume, along with a make-up kit, and explained what I was to do. The costume was standard-issue: a baggy clown suit with a scarlet wig. I was also given a pair of the sneakers to wear. Imprinted on them was the logo: a capering clown.

As for my duties, I was told to circulate among the attendees. Costumed as Mr. Sneakers, I would be a roving advertisement for the brand. Any antics that I wished to engage in would be fine. However, I was not to speak—that was important, I was told. The comedy was to be strictly pantomime.

I suited up and began to roam. Sales booths occupied an entire floor of the hotel, promoting every imaginable type of shoe. I wandered about, a conspicuous figure in my non-business attire. Getting into the role, I waved at people; mugged and cavorted; examined the shoes on display, like a prospective buyer. At one point I even picked up a fire extinguisher and pretended to spray people. Periodically, I would return to our booth and perform my antics there—strictly adhering to my mandate of silence. I was having a good time. I *was* Mr. Sneakers.

Then my circulating came to an abrupt halt. As I strolled about, I was stopped by two trade-fair officials. They asked me what company I was with. Mindful of my instructions—and staying in character—I remained silent and shrugged. The officials persisted. Where were my employers located? they wanted to know. My response was to gesture vaguely. Whereupon, they told me that if I did not lead them to my employers, I would be arrested.

There are limits to the loyalty of a temporary employee. Moreover, the prospect of being arrested—and being led off in a clown suit—was unsettling. So I beckoned for them to follow me, and led them to the Mr. Sneakers booth.

And I learned now why I had been instructed to limit my comedic efforts to pantomime. The rules of the fair forbade any advertising beyond the immediate area of one's booth. But my employers had imagined that, if their roaming mascot refrained from speaking or passing out printed matter, they would be in compliance with the rules.

I spent the remainder of the fair at our booth, seeking to draw attention to its display of sneakers. I still waved and mugged at people; but no longer was I a roving madcap. Mr. Sneakers had been grounded.

Late in the afternoon the scores of exhibitors began to pack up; and I was told I could go. I climbed out of the suit and washed off the make-up. My employers paid me in cash, and told me to keep the pair of sneakers I had worn. Those dollars would soon be spent. But the sneakers would serve as a memento of my brief employment as a mascot.

•

My next venture into show business came a few years later. It was as a magician.

I was living in Cambridge, Massachusetts, and working at a bookstore. And the idea came to me to put together a magic act. Why not outfit myself as a magician and perform at children's parties? It seemed a cool thing to do—both artistic and enterprising.

So I began by visiting Jack's Joke Shop. Located in downtown Boston, Jack's was a prankster's paradise—dribble glasses, itching powder, whoopie cushions. But a section of the shop was devoted to magic tricks. I bought a bagful.*

Next, I went to a costume shop and bought a wizard's cap. It resembled the one Mickey Mouse had worn as the sorcerer's apprentice. At a thrift shop I picked up a black jacket—one with deep pockets that could be loaded with tricks. I sent away for magic catalogs. And eventually I was ready to perform.

I had decided to adopt "Professor Solomon" as a stage name. I printed up business cards that identified me as such, that gave my phone number, and that purported to describe my show. My sole form of advertising, the card read as follows:

HAVING A CHILDREN'S PARTY?
PROFESSOR SOLOMON THE MAGICIAN

> With card tricks, coin tricks, egg tricks, sudden personal disappearances, ring tricks, the gorilla transformation, a snowstorm, rope tricks, telepathy, Abraham Mlinkin (the college-bowl star penny), wine-to-pretzels, an elephant produced in your living room, floating (Professor Solomon will float in mid-air), firebolts, cigarettes from ears, the Chinese vase, a vanishing glass, applause from nowhere, the famous apple of knowledge, a Rabbi from a hat, escapes, etc.

Actually, the card was a literary exercise. Few of those tricks were included in the show (or even existed). Still, I did offer a variety of illusions. I made a selected card appear inside a corked bottle. I produced colorful silks. I caused a glass of milk to disappear. I pulled a red, white, and blue flagpole from my hat. (This telescoping pole was my most expensive trick.) I linked rings and read minds. And I did in fact produce that elephant (or at least its trunk, protruding from my hat).

---

* Jack's was founded in 1922, and billed itself as the World's Oldest Joke Shop. Sadly, this venerable institution closed its doors in 2006.

For my debut performance I had worn the wizard's cap. But it was silly-looking, I decided. So I returned to the costume shop and bought a top hat. I also sent away for a magician's cape. (It had a secret feature that enabled all sorts of mischief.) Thus did I upgrade my look to that of a classical stage magician.

During the course of my career, I performed less than a dozen times. Some of these were paid performances, for children at birthday parties; others were *pro bono,* for friends and relatives. My repertoire was limited, as was my technical proficiency; but children seemed to enjoy the show. I recall the amazement of one child when I pulled a banana from her ear, and her further amazement when I let her hold it: a *rubber* banana! I entertained at a party for members of the Harvard Philosophy Club. And visiting my parents in Ohio, I performed at a family gathering.

And I had one fiasco, at Phillips Brooks House. This was the center at Harvard for volunteerism and community service. The girlfriend of one of those philosophers was a volunteer there; and she had asked me to perform for a group of disadvantaged youths. I was glad to oblige.

Upon arriving at Phillips Brooks, I set up my show in its social hall; donned my top hat and cape; and watched as the boys and girls filed in. They were middle-school students from a working-class neighborhood in Cambridge. As I should have expected, they proved to be a difficult audience—boisterous and unruly; and the show went badly from the start. I was distracted by their behavior. Tricks didn't work—jokes fell flat—I failed to connect.

My card trick, for example, was a disaster. The trick was a simple one that made clever use of a piece of Scotch tape. A selected card is returned to the deck; and the deck is hurled against the wall. The cards fall to the floor. But the selected card is left stuck on the wall! Alas, on this occasion it failed to stick. I made a lame excuse; and I had to gather up the cards and hurl them twice more, before the card stuck to the wall.

There was a mishap, too, with my disappearing glass of

milk. It had disappeared without a hitch, to a hiding place beneath the table. But then I knocked it over with my foot. As milk flowed out into plain sight, cries of derision filled the hall. Indeed, from the start I had been subjected to cat-calls, wisecracks, hooting, and derogatory remarks. "You stink!" one of the youths had called out. (He had a point.) I was barely able to finish the show.

But the crowning indignity was yet to come. When the show was over, I laid down my wand and thanked everyone for coming. And I was chatting with the volunteer, when a boy came over, snatched my wand, and ran off with it. Instinctively, I chased after him. I caught up with the thief, grabbed him, and—forcibly—retrieved my wand.

Finally, the youths were led away. Relieved that my ordeal was over, I packed up. And I left the building with the volunteer, who had offered me a ride home.

But as we walked to her car, I was ambushed. Lying in wait for me was that boy whom I had grabbed. Out for revenge, he ran up, kicked me in the shin, and fled.

The Davenport Brothers

On a spring afternoon in 1895, Henry Ridgely Evans approached a theatrical boarding-house on Thirteenth Street in Washington. And he spotted the magician whom he had come to visit. Harry Kellar was standing on the sidewalk out front, conversing with two men. One of them, recalls Evans in *The Old and the New Magic,* was tall, slim, and elegantly dressed, in a Prince Albert coat, gray trousers, and slouch hat. The other was "a fat fellow with a rubicund face. He was habited in a checked suit —the biggest checks I ever saw. It resembled nothing less than a gigantic checker-board."

Kellar introduced him to Ira Davenport, in the Prince Albert coat, and William Fay, in the checked suit. The two men shook hands with Evans and exchanged a few words with him. Then they took leave of Kellar and passed into the boarding-house.

> That was my first and last meeting with Ira Davenport, the eldest of the world-famous Davenport Brothers, spirit-mediums, so called, who in the heyday of their career caused such a sensation in America and Europe. It seemed strange to me to see Kellar, the exposer of mediumship, in Ira's company, talking so glibly and acting so friendly. By rights, they should have been at daggers drawn. Kellar had practically ruined the medium's business. But in the old days, Kellar had traveled with the Davenports as an assistant, and was much liked by them....Kellar and Davenport and Fay were having a jovial time when I saw them. They were doubtless exchanging the secrets of the trade and heartily enjoying themselves.

By a curious coincidence, Kellar and Davenport were appearing in Washington at the same time—the magician at the National Theatre; the medium at Willard's Hall—

and both were exhibiting a spirit cabinet. Kellar, however, presented his cabinet as an illusion—an entertainment—a conjuring effect. Davenport and Fay, on the other hand, billed their show as a séance. Otherworldly spirits, they claimed, were manifesting themselves inside the cabinet.

Evans attended both shows. He even participated in Kellar's, coming on stage as part of an audience committee. But while Keller played to full houses, Davenport and Fay drew meager audiences; and after a few days, they closed their show and cancelled plans for a tour. The pair had sought to revive an act that, a quarter-century earlier, had brought fame to the Davenport brothers. But the public had since grown skeptical about spirits, and had lost interest in them.

Ira Davenport had emerged from retirement, hoping to revive the act, with Fay as a replacement for his late brother. Disappointed, he returned now to his home in Mayville, New York. And on a porch overlooking Lake Chautauqua, he sat in a rocking chair—sipping the lemonades that his wife brought out to him, and savoring the memories of an improbable career.

Beginnings in Buffalo

That career had begun in Buffalo, at a table in the home of the Davenport family. The father, mother, and three children—Ira (fifteen), William (thirteen), and Elizabeth (ten)—had decided to conduct a séance. The Fox sisters had become a sensation with their manifestations; and the Davenport children, encouraged by their father, wanted to see if they could elicit similar phenomena.*

* The Fox sisters of Hydesville, a hamlet ninety miles from Buffalo, had been instrumental in the creation of Spiritualism. In 1848, fifteen-year-old Maggie and twelve-year-old Kate had claimed to be in contact with spirits: rapping sounds were answering their questions! Traveling about, the girls conducted séances that brought them renown as mediums, and that popularized the

So that night, in February 1855, the family extinguished the lights and sat themselves at a table in the parlor. They rested their hands on it; and in solemn silence, awaited a sign from the spirits.

Suddenly, the table shook. It rocked back and forth. And mysterious sounds began to be heard. Crackles—thumps—raps, like someone knocking on wood. Finally, *questions were answered by the raps.* The Davenports had contacted the spirits! How else to explain these strange goings-on? Excited by their success, the family continued the séance late into the night.

In the weeks that followed, they conducted more sessions. Joining them now in the parlor were neighbors and strangers. For word had spread about the ghostly phenomena that were taking place—induced, apparently, by the mediumistic powers of the children. The phenomena grew more varied. In addition to thumps and raps, eerie voices were heard; musical instruments flew about in the dark; and flashes of light illumined the parlor.

The manifestations became a topic of heated debate in Buffalo, with skeptics denouncing them as trickery. And the demand to witness them was such that the father rented a hall. There he held public séances, charging an entrance fee.

As the seats filled each night, it became evident to Davenport that the spirits could provide him with a livelihood. And he recalled how the Fox sisters had gone on tour

---

idea of communication with departed souls. Spiritualism soon became a major movement in America.

Forty years later Maggie—now impoverished and alcoholic (communing, alas, with liquid spirits)—took the stage before a packed house at the New York Academy of Music, and confessed that the rappings had been a hoax. She demonstrated how she and Kate had produced the sounds—by cracking the joints of their toes.

A year later she recanted her confession. The rappings had indeed been the work of spirits, declared Maggie, but a $1500 payment had induced her to say otherwise. Her contradictory claims prompted a controversy that has lasted to the present day.

as mediums. A chemist named James Mapes encouraged him to do likewise:

> In the autumn of 1855, Davenport received a letter from Prof. Mapes of New Jersey, to the effect that he, Mapes, was coming on to Buffalo, expressly to satisfy himself, by ocular demonstration, whether the wonders reported of the circle were real or fanciful, false or true. Davenport wrote back saying, "Come on: every facility you require in order to a candid and fair investigation shall be accorded and afforded you." Mapes went, saw, explored, tested, and finally gave in that the half had not been told. He was delighted with the results obtained, and from that hour in him the Davenport family had a true, firm, constant, and unswerving friend, and so he remained. That visit satisfied him completely; and it proved, eventually, to be the most important visit, both to the family and the world, that they had theretofore received, inasmuch as from that visit dates the resolution of the family to travel and display their marvels to the full, broad gaze of the world at large.*

Finally, Davenport quit his job as a policeman; his sons, who delivered newspapers, quit theirs. And the three of them headed east, intent on displaying those marvels. Their initial stop would be Rochester, where the Fox sisters had given their first public exhibition of the rapping sounds. With thumps, mysterious voices, and instruments flying about in the dark, the Davenports intended to outdo them.

Rochester

Rochester was an industrial center, with a profusion of flour mills. But it was also a hotbed of reform and radicalism. Abolitionism, Spiritualism, mesmeric healing, women's

* Pascal Beverly Randolph, *The Davenport Brothers, The World-Renowned Spiritual Mediums: Their Biography, and Adventures in Europe and America* (1869). The book is a hagiography, though by the time it was published, Randolph had ceased to believe in the genuineness of their manifestations.

rights, temperance—all these were flourishing in Rochester in 1855. Six years earlier, the Fox sisters had conducted séances in the city; and eager to hear the rappings, hundreds of people had crowded into Corinthian Hall. (Its acoustics were the best of any hall in America—ideal for hearing rappings.) Now the Davenport brothers were stopping in Rochester. Managed by their father, they too conducted séances—creating a stir that rivaled that of the sisters. Spirits manifesting themselves! The antics of these "disembodied intelligences" are described by a witness:

> The room was darkened; and, almost immediately, there commenced a series of demonstrations.... The trumpet was repeatedly spoken through at an elevation which precluded the idea of any one of the auditors or mediums using the same. The instruments and bells floated around the room, keeping up an incessant vibration and ding-dong; being frequently lowered, and brought in contact with the limbs, &c., of those present, sometimes so forcibly as to leave a painful impression of several minutes' duration. The hat of the writer was taken from his head.... On the appearance of a light, we proceeded to search for the hat, which had so strangely left us, and found it on a seat on the other side of the room.*

From Rochester they continued on to Troy and other towns, conducting séances in each. But their destination was New York City. There Professor Mapes had been spreading the word about these successors to the Fox sisters. Moreover, a business-agent had alerted the press and engaged a hall.

The Bowery

"When they reached the city," reports Randolph, "the greatest excitement ensued, and hundreds of people ran wild with anxiety to see these marvelous young Thau-

* From a letter, quoted by Randolph, that "a gentleman of Rochester" sent to a newspaper.

maturgii." Davenport senior and his sons checked into a hotel. And while preparations were being made for the exhibition, they paid a social call. For Professor Mapes, their staunchest supporter, had invited them to pay a visit to his home in New Jersey.

On a wintry afternoon the Davenports took a train to Newark. Mapes welcomed them to his home and introduced them to his wife and daughters. Other guests arrived; there was food and socializing. And a séance was held:

> When evening set in, the professor invited them and his guests into the parlors, two in number, with folding-doors between. To the lintels of these doors, Mapes had suspended a snare-drum, beyond reach of any save one who stood upon a chair. The drumsticks and other instruments were placed upon a table, at which table sat the media [i.e., the two mediums]....All being ready, the word was given, and out went the lights, and away went the instruments all over the rooms, thrumming, thumping, squalling....But the most curious things about it was, that the drumsticks not only thumped upon the drum heartily, but alternated on Mapes's head, gently, softly, and discreetly, so as not to injure his cranium. (Randolph, *The Davenport Brothers*)

When asked if it could play on the piano, the spirit did so, filling the darkened parlors with a "most exquisite melody."

Two days later their exhibition opened at Union Hall, an assembly room on the Bowery. Eighty persons attended. The majority of them were Spiritualists, come to see the spirits in action. Presiding over the event was Professor Mapes. He introduced Ira and William, who were seated at a table, and described their mediumistic powers. Then, with lengths of rope, he tied them to their chairs. For the brothers had agreed to be bound during the séance. The idea was to allay suspicions that they engineered the manifestations—that is to say, practiced deception.

After binding them, Mapes sat down near the table. On it were a bell, a speaking-horn, a guitar and other instruments. The lights were extinguished, leaving the hall in total darkness and evoking a murmur of anticipation.

Soon the phenomena began. Instruments sounded as they flew about in the dark. Mysterious voices were heard. Rappings conveyed messages. The audience had come for a show; and the spirits—as energetic as ever—did not disappoint them.

And while Mapes believed these doings to be the work of spirits, he did experience a moment of doubt. The guitar had flown off the table and landed in his lap. Instinctively, he reached out in the dark—and felt a human figure. "I believed [it] to be young Ira Davenport, whom I examined from head to foot...but whom I could not hold, as he, or it slipped through my hands, or melted away."

Yet when the lights came on, Ira was still bound to his chair. Initially, Mapes was perplexed; but he was able finally to make sense of what had happened. The incident "convinced me of two new facts; and these are, first, that the invisibles really incarnate themselves from elements emanating in great part from the persons of the media; and second, that, in the majority of cases, these special incarnations are precise and exact counterparts of the medium."

In other words, *the spirit had emanated from Ira.* It was his etheric double, concluded Mapes—a second self that he was able to project. And what had initially seemed to be a discovery of deception, had in fact been a privileged moment.*

The brothers remained in New York for three weeks, conducting daily séances. Their father then took them back to Buffalo; and the séances continued. It was now standard

* In his biography of the Davenport brothers, Randolph not only accepts that Ira could project himself, but claims to possess a similar power: "The writer himself has often been seen in two places at one time, and, indeed, has the power of pneuma-projection to a great extent, being able to appear at points over a hundred miles distant from his body, but only when in peculiar states of mental and bodily health; that is, when unhappy, grieving, sorrowful, and in low health."

practice for Ira and William to be tied to their chairs. Thus restrained, they could not be accused of faking the manifestations. (Or so it was assumed, by those unfamiliar with the resourcefulness of magicians.) Moreover, tying them to their chairs added to the theatricality of the séance.

And it was about to become even more theatrical. For the Davenports were building a cabinet for the spirits.

Cabinet

The spirit cabinet was a wooden box. It was six feet high, seven feet wide, and two-and-a-half feet deep. To allay suspicions of a trapdoor, it was mounted on saw-horses. Three doors—one with a small aperture—opened at the front. Inside were three benches. And hanging on the rear wall were musical instruments. The purpose of the cabinet was to provide the spirits with a venue.

It became the centerpiece of their séances. Ira and William would sit inside, facing one another. Volunteers tied them to the benches; bound their hands and feet; and affirmed that the brothers could not get loose. Then the doors of the cabinet were shut; and the lights in the hall were dimmed.

Almost immediately, the spirits began to manifest themselves. Formerly, they had made their presence known in the darkness of the hall; now they did so in that of the cabinet. From inside sounded the twanging of a guitar, the bleating of a horn, the jingling of a tambourine. And at one point, a spectral hand emerged from the aperture and rang a bell!

When the doors were reopened, the brothers were still tied to the benches. Their hands and feet were still bound; and the instruments were still on the wall, out of reach. Clearly, a supernatural agency had been responsible for the musical sounds. The doors were closed; and the manifestations continued.

Then Davenport senior called for a volunteer. Who would be willing, he asked, to join his sons in the cabinet and confirm that no trickery was involved? A volunteer came forward, climbed into the cabinet, and sat between

Ira and William. He was told to place a hand on each of them: any movements would thus be detected. And the doors were shut.

Once again musical sounds were heard. When the doors were reopened, the volunteer seemed dazed. On his head was the tambourine. His cravat had been removed and tied around Ira's neck; his spectacles were now on William. He reported that the brothers had not moved—and that spirits had pulled on his hair and pinched his nose!

Their exhibitions were divided now into two parts, referred to as the cabinet séance and the dark séance. For the latter, the cabinet was rolled aside; and chairs were placed directly in front of the audience. The brothers were tied to the chairs. The lights were extinguished. And the shenanigans continued.

The spirit cabinet, says Randolph, drew large audiences:

> [The cabinet] created such a stir in Buffalo and the regions round about, that an entirely new class of people, most of whom had theretofore ignored spiritism in all shapes, became interested and attracted to the circles; and consequently...the room was literally crammed and jammed with people long hours before the time to commence the session.

Encouraged by the response to their cabinet, the Davenports began to tour with it. Beginning in 1856 and for the next eight years, the brothers traveled extensively. Managed initially by their father, and later by others, Ira and William had become itinerant showmen.

Harvard Professors

The Davenport brothers were a popular attraction. But they were also controversial; and not infrequently, they encountered opposition. While many believed in their powers, others deemed them to be frauds. They were accused of being magicians—"jugglers" who posed as mediums in order to fleece the credulous.

Opponents of Spiritualism sought to expose them. In Richmond, Indiana, a physician had sneaked into the cabinet, earlier in the day, and applied creosote oil to the violin. After the manifestations, he claimed to smell creosote on the brothers' hands—evidence that they, and not spirits, had been playing on the instruments. Angry spectators stormed the stage, demanding a refund. "Their box, horns, violins, banjoes, etc., were pretty roughly kicked about," reports the Richmond *Palladium.* The Davenports had to flee via a back door.

And in Boston, their powers were tested by a committee of Harvard professors. The Boston *Courier* had offered a prize of $500, to any medium who elicited a manifestation that was deemed genuine by this committee. The Fox sisters had already been tested, says Randolph; and "the professors made no other discovery than that there were 'unaccountable noises'—a discovery which any country bumpkin was equally competent to make." Now they turned their attention to the Davenport brothers.

The head of the committee was Benjamin Peirce, professor of mathematics and astronomy. The Davenports had agreed—reluctantly—to let Peirce join them inside the cabinet. Thus placed, he would endeavor to detect any trickery. A reporter from the *Courier* witnessed the test:

> The boys took their place, and were carefully tied with stout cords by direction of the Committee.... Prof. Peirce entered the box and took his seat on the back side of it, between the boys, they sitting at each end facing each other. The Professor gathered, at once, all the musical instruments, consisting of two tambourines, a fiddle, a banjo, and a tin horn, between his legs.
>
> It was an uncommonly striking spectacle.... Before the last jet of gas was turned off, the aspect of Prof. Peirce, looking out from the shadows of his tabernacle, with the spiritual youngsters on each side of him, and vigilantly guarding the implements which were soon to be toned by the supernatural orchestra, was something truly pictorial to behold.

After ten minutes the lamps were re-lit and the doors were opened. There had been no playing on the instruments—no manifestations of the spirits. Peirce emerged from the cabinet with nothing to report. Apparently, his presence (and his guarding of the instruments) had dissuaded the spirits from manifesting themselves.*

* In *A Biography of the Brothers Davenport* (1864), T. L. Nichols—a British physician, Spiritualist, and supporter of the Davenports—offers a different version of what transpired. According to Nichols, Peirce had secretly brought some phosphorus into the cabinet with him. Once the manifestations had begun, he ignited the phosphorus—intending to illuminate the cabinet. Instead, he "half suffocated himself and the boys with its fumes." And when the doors were opened, says Nichols, he had a tambourine on his head. Moreover, the spirits had untied the brothers. "And the ropes were found twisted around the neck of the watchful

The $500 prize was awarded to none of the mediums. Their powers had been tested and found wanting. "Spiritism shown as it is!" proclaimed the *Courier.* And the newspaper reported the results of the testing:

> Nothing was done, by the most famous mediums which could be collected, in the country, far and near, except a little rapping by the Foxes, easily traceable to their persons and easily done by others without the pretence of spirits; not a table or piano lifted or anything moved a single hair's breadth; not a bell rung, nor an instrument played upon; nor any phenomenon or manifestation exhibited or even attempted. So ends this ridiculous and infamous imposture.

But the mediums had an explanation for their failures. They insisted that the "negative force" emanating from the skeptical professors had kept the spirits away.

Cooper Institute

They may have failed to elicit any manifestations for the professors; but the Davenports continued to do so for those attending their exhibitions. And by 1864 they had become the best-known, and most controversial, mediums in America. In April of that year they arrived in New York, for an engagement at the Cooper Institute (where Lincoln, four years earlier, had delivered his celebrated speech on slavery). On the opening night, Spiritualists and skeptics alike

---

Professor Peirce!"

Which version is to be credited? Nichols, it is true, got much of the information for his biography directly from Ira and William. Yet which is more reliable—the recollections of a pair of showmen, which are likely to be embellished (or even fabricated), or the account of an eyewitness reporter? Both Nichols and Randolph (the latter having based his biography on interviews with the father) must be read with caution. The Davenports are dubious sources for facts about themselves.

took seats in the Great Hall. On the platform sat the cabinet, like an altar awaiting its priests. Three musicians—a pianist, a violinist, and a cornetist—provided music for the congregants.

Among those attending was the Reverend J. B. Ferguson, a clergyman from Nashville. Ferguson had been the pastor of a major church there; but he had resigned his pulpit, after becoming a believer in Spiritualism. What Ferguson witnessed in the Great Hall that night would strengthen his belief:

> When we came to the place of meeting—the large lecture-room of the Cooper Institute, the largest in New York city—we found some thousands assembled. The entertainment—for such it may properly be called—opened, and a committee was chosen to secure the young men in the cabinet and report to the audience what occurred. I need not describe the manifestations, or their effect on the audience, as the New York papers gave graphic reports at the time, and have indulged in tiresome repetitions since. It is enough to say that I was convinced that the Davenports were no jugglers [illusionists], and that the displays of power through them admitted of no explanation according to any known estimate of natural laws. (From a statement quoted by Nichols)

Weary of war news, readers welcomed those reports. The *World* described the brothers, who were no longer boys:

> The Davenport Brothers, known throughout the country as spiritual mediums, or by unbelievers as sleight-of-hand performers, appeared last evening at the Cooper Institute; and it was announced by advertisement that startling wonders, mysterious displays, and unaccountable manifestations would take place in their presence. ["Unaccountable manifestations" was their standard disclaimer; no mention of spirits appeared in their advertising.] The fame of their feats of *diablerie* had preceded them, and the large hall was crowded....They looked remarkably like each other in almost every particular, both quite handsome, and between twenty-five and thirty years old, with rather long, curly

> black hair.... They were dressed in black, with dress coats, one wearing a watch-chain.

The *Herald* was equally non-committal as to the nature of their abilities:

> Cooper Institute was crowded last night by a fashionable as well as a promiscuous [diverse] audience, to witness the performance of the Davenport Brothers—a couple of young men who have created a marked sensation wherever they have exhibited their feats. Their performances have been variously ascribed to the powers of Spiritualism, and to legerdemain, or sleight-of-hand.

The Davenports performed at the Cooper Institute for eleven days. They also held private séances: for the editor of the *Herald;* for the mayor and city council; and for John Morrissey. Morrissey was a notorious figure in New York. He was a boxing champion (the sport was illegal); the leader of a gang called the Dead Rabbits; and a vote-getter for Boss Tweed. ("As an organizer of repeaters," Tweed said of him, "he had no superior.") In 1866 these credentials would win him election to the U.S. House of Representatives, where he told his colleagues: "I have reached the height of my ambition. I have been a wharf rat, chicken thief, prizefighter, gambler, and member of Congress." At their private séance, Morrissey and his cronies placed bets on the proceedings:

> John Morrissey, the pugilist, solicited the Davenports to give a sitting to a company of noted fast characters, at a down-town gambling-house. As the request was accompanied by the needful fifty dollars, an afternoon was given to them, and, although several thousands of dollars changed hands on the result of the experiments, they expressed themselves delighted and confounded by the wonders they had witnessed. The Brothers testify to the good behavior of the gamblers, and say, though they [the gamblers] resorted to every method to detect fraud, and tied them more skillfully than they were ever tied before, they were subjected

> to less severe usage than is customary with a company of clergymen and physicians.*

Yet at least one clergyman had no doubts about the Davenports. The Reverend Ferguson had been profoundly affected by the manifestations—so much so that he attended every performance at the Cooper Institute. He also paid a personal visit to the brothers, introducing himself and discussing Spiritualism. Apparently, Ira and William took a liking to Ferguson (and realized that he would confer respectability on their exhibitions). For they asked him to travel with them as a lecturer. Ferguson had been offered the pulpit at a church in Brooklyn; but he decided instead to join the Davenports. "I did so," he explained, "because I was fully convinced that the phenomena which occurred in the presence of the Brothers were a part of the supramundane evidence given to this age."

The brothers themselves had become a phenomenon. Their séances at the Cooper Institute, says Nichols, "were the culmination and crowning triumphs of their ten years' American experience." And a new phase of their career was about to begin, on the other side of the Atlantic. There they would acquire wider renown, financial well-being, and wives.

Adah Menken

Adah Menken (1835?–1868) was the most acclaimed, highly-paid, and notorious actress of her day. The acclaim was due to her beauty, more than her acting ability, and to an instinct for self-promotion. (She was one of the first actresses to publicize herself with photographs.) The notoriety was due to her unconventionality, and to her role in a melodrama called *Mazeppa*.

Menken concocted exotic, and conflicting, tales as to her

* Orrin Abbott, *The Davenport Brothers: Their History, Travels, and Manifestations* (1864)

origins. But she was probably born in Memphis, as Ada McCord, and raised in New Orleans. By the age of twenty-two, she was performing with a theatre company. And she had married Alexander Menken, a musician who served as her manager. He was the son of a prominent Jewish family in Cincinnati; and Adah embraced (though never formally converted to) Judaism. In Ohio and elsewhere, the young actress found work. She also wrote poems and essays—many of them on Jewish themes—that were published in the Cincinnati *Israelite.*

In February 1858, for a production of *Macbeth* in Nashville, she was cast as Lady Macbeth. James Murdoch, a noted tragedian, was playing Macbeth. The day of the first performance, Menken approached him with a confession: she knew nothing about the part. But she could handle it, Menken insisted, and could learn the lines in a few hours. Murdoch, who had an eye for the ladies, agreed to tutor her in the role. Years later, he would recall:

> I found her to be a mere novice, and not at all qualified for the important position to which she aspired. But she was anxious to improve and willing to be taught. A woman of great personal attractions, she made herself a great favourite. She dashed at everything in tragedy and comedy with a reckless disregard of consequences until, at length, with some degree of trepidation, she paused before the character of Lady Macbeth.

But on stage that night, Menken whispered to him that she had forgotten her lines.

> From that point Macbeth ceased to be the guilty thane and became a mere prompter in Scotch kilts and tartans. For the rest of the scene I gave the lady the words.*

Later that year, at a theatre in Newark, Menken starred in *The Unprotected Female.* She was billed as "The Accom-

* Quoted in *Mazeppa: The Lives, Loves and Legends of Adah Isaacs Menken* by Wolf Mankowitz (1982)

plished Actress, The Sterling Tragedienne, The Popular Comedienne, The Enchanting Songstress, The Bewitching Danseuse." This may have been puffery; but the curtain seemed to be rising on a promising career.

As for the direction of that career, she would follow Murdoch's advice. He had counseled her to seek out some "sensational spectacle" in which "your fine figure and pretty face will show to the same advantage as the prosperous curves of, say, Madame Celeste" (a scantily-clad French dancer). In the summer of 1861, such a spectacle came along. It was called *Mazeppa, or the Wild Horse of Tartary.*

Mazeppa was a three-act play based on a poem by Lord Byron. It was being revived by Captain John Smith, at his Green Street Theatre in Albany. But when ticket sales proved disappointing, Smith had an idea. In the climactic scene, Mazeppa—a Tartar prince—is taken captive, stripped naked, and strapped to a horse. This "fiery untamed steed of Tartary" then bears him off into the mountains. Smith's innovative idea was to have *a woman* play the part of Mazeppa.

He offered the part to Menken, who by now was appearing regularly in theatres in New York. (She had also divorced Alexander Menken and married a boxing champion.) At first she demurred—though not on account of the nudity. Rather, a female Mazeppa seemed an absurdity. But Smith was persuasive. When he described the controversy that the nudity would provoke, and the resulting publicity for whoever took the part, she signed on.

Rehearsals began. Menken was given a crash-course in horsemanship. In that climactic scene, the horse—bearing the actress—would climb a scaffolding in front of painted mountains. On her first attempt to get onto the horse, she was thrown.*

---

* Several times during her career as Mazeppa, Menken was thrown from the horse. On one of those occasions (the story goes), she landed on a stagehand. "Is there a doctor in the house?" the stage manager called out to the audience. Many hands went up. But when he added that the injured party was the stagehand, the hands all went down.

And she acquired her costume: a flesh-colored body-stocking that, in dim light, would make her appear to be nude. Smith had new posters printed. They showed a black stallion rearing up, with a voluptuous—and nearly naked—woman lashed to its back. The Tartar prince had undergone a radical transformation.

And while there were more pressing stories to be covered—the first shots of the Civil War had been fired, and states were seceding from the Union—reporters flocked to Albany for the reopening of the show. Introduced by her press agent as "one of the greatest and most courageous artistes of our theatre," Menken gave interviews in her hotel suite. She wore a short skirt and loose blouse. And she was lounging on a tiger-skin, drinking champagne, and smoking a cigarette—relishing the role of an uninhibited artiste.

On opening night the theatre was sold-out, with hundreds standing. Mankowitz describes the moment that everyone had come to see:

> When, partially shielded by actors, Menken performed the first public striptease act ever witnessed in a theatre, the audience was almost religiously silent. Then, in her invisible tights and flimsy tunic, she was revealed by the light of the flickering torches, and the great shocked and excited gasp assured Smith that he had, indeed, secured his place in the history of the American Theatre. An American audience had seen, for the first time, a naked lady on the stage.... that audience, after its momentary stillness and its great gasp of shock, rose to its feet and hailed Mazeppa with a great roar of applause and protest. That deliciously thrilling and purely animal sound was to echo through the remainder of Adah Isaacs Menken's sadly short but always sensational life.

Captain Smith had a hit—a financial bonanza, thanks to its inspired casting. Immediately, he arranged to move the production to New York. It opened there a week later, at the Broadway Theatre. On opening night, Menken was escorted to the theatre by Walt Whitman, her friend and poetry mentor. (They had met at Pfaff's Tavern, a gathering place for bohemians.) Again, the house was sold-out. And *Mazeppa* —an undistinguished melodrama—would go on to set box-office records.

It was the turning point in Menken's career. Almost overnight, she became the first celebrity actress. During the next three years, she would appear in theatres around the country—most often in productions of *Mazeppa,* but in other plays as well. She was featured, for example, in *Three Fast Women,* one of the first musicals.

In the summer of 1863, with eight trunks and a new husband—a journalist had replaced the pugilist—she sailed from New York to San Francisco. (The voyage involved two steamers, with a connecting train across the Isthmus of Panama.) She had a contract to star in *Mazeppa* at the San Francisco Opera House.

The initial run of sixteen performances were sold-out before opening night. Mark Twain saw the show and wrote a review. He describes Menken as a "finely formed woman," and takes note of the horse:

> They strap Mazeppa on his back...and the horse goes cantering up-stairs over the painted mountains, through tinted clouds of theatrical mist, in a brisk exciting way, with the wretched victim he bears unconsciously digging her heels into his hams, in the agony of her sufferings, to make him go faster. Then a tempest of applause bursts forth, and the curtain falls. The fierce old circus horse carries his prisoner around through the back part of the theatre, behind the scenery, and although assailed at every step by the savage wolves of the desert, he makes his way at last to his dear old home in Tartary down by the foot lights, and beholds once more, O, gods! the familiar faces of the fiddlers in the orchestra. The noble old steed is happy, then, but poor Mazeppa is insensible.

After an extended—and highly profitable—stay in California, Menken traveled to Nevada. There she performed for a month in the mining town of Virginia City. As

Mazeppa was stripped, lashed to the horse, and borne off into the mountains, the miners cheered wildly and (legend has it) tossed silver nuggets onto the stage.

But more refined audiences awaited "The Menken" (as she had been dubbed). In April 1864, with her dresser Minnie and 28 pieces of luggage, the actress boarded a ship and set sail for Great Britain.

London

After their stay in New York, the Davenport brothers spent three months on the road, hauling their cabinet from town to town. Accompanying them were Palmer, their new manager; the Reverend Ferguson, their new presenter; and William Fay. Originally from Buffalo, the 24-year-old Fay had become their general assistant. He had started out as a ticket-taker, and now had a role in the dark séance. (Prior to joining the Davenports, he had performed as a mind-reader.) Ferguson's role was to deliver a lecture. He also served as a representative of the brothers, who rarely spoke during the séance. Instead, says Henry Ridgely Evans, "they presented a calm, sphinx-like imperturbability, which nothing seemed to ruffle."

The séances were still drawing audiences in these towns. But an ambitious plan was in the works—one that would build on the success at the Cooper Institute. And in late August, the Davenports, along with Palmer, Ferguson, Fay, and Fay's wife Eliza, embarked upon an adventure. The company loaded their bags, cabinet, musical instruments, ropes, and scrapbook of press clippings onto the *Britannia,* and set sail for Great Britain. A spirit, claimed the Davenports, had directed them to do so.

By the middle of September they were in London. An astute publicist, Palmer began by arranging a series of private séances. Invited to these were journalists and "persons of scientific, literary, or social distinction," says Nichols (who was among those who attended). The first was held at the home of Dion Boucicault, a popular actor and playwright. Accounts of the event appeared in several newspapers. The *Morning Post* reported:

EXTRAORDINARY MANIFESTATIONS

Yesterday evening, in the front drawing-room of a house in the immediate neighbourhood of Portland-place, a select number of persons were invited to witness some strange manifestations which took place in the presence, if not by the agency, of three gentlemen lately arrived from America. The party consisted of two brothers named Davenport, twenty-four and twenty-five years of age, and a Mr. Fay, a gentleman born in the States, but we believe of German origin. They are accompanied by Mr. H. D. Palmer, a gentleman long and favourably known in New York in connection with operatic matters, and by a Dr. Ferguson, who explains the nature of the manifestations about to be presented, but who does not venture to give any explanation of them. It should be stated at the outset that the trio, who appear to be gifted in so extraordinary a manner, do not lay claim to any particular physical, psychological, or moral power. All they assert is that in their presence certain physical manifestations take place. The spectator is, of course, at liberty to draw any inference he pleases. They invite the most critical examination (compatible with certain conditions to be observed), and those who witness the manifestations are at liberty to take all needful precautions against fraud or deception.

The party invited to witness the manifestations last night consisted of some twelve or fourteen individuals, all of whom are admitted to be of considerable distinction in the various professions with which they are connected.

The article goes on to describe the cabinet séance. The brothers seated themselves inside the cabinet. It had been set up amid the elegant furnishings of the Boucicault drawing-room. Volunteers bound the brothers. The cabinet doors were shut; the lights were turned low; and the manifestations began. The guitar, tambourine, and bell sounded from within. Hands emerged from the aperture. (These hands were "ghostly enough to elicit a set of little awe-struck ejaculations from the ladies present," reported the *Standard.*) When the doors were opened, Ira and William were revealed to be still securely bound. Or so it seemed.

Equally mystifying was the second portion of the evening's entertainment—the dark séance, for which the cabinet was no longer required. The brothers sat directly in front of the spectators. Volunteers tied them to their chairs. A correspondent from the *Times* (who would receive a minor injury) describes what happened next:

> When the lights had been extinguished, and as we were all seated round the room with hands joined, at the request of the lecturer, a most extraordinary "manifestation" took place. The air was filled with the sound of instruments which we had seen laid upon a table, but which now seemed to be flying about the room, playing as they went, without the smallest respect to the heads of the visitors. Now a bell jingled close to your ear, now a guitar was struck immediately over your head, while every now and then a cold wind passed across the faces of the whole party. Sometimes a smart blow was administered, sometimes the knee was patted by a mysterious hand; divers shrieks from the members of the company indicating the side on which the more tangible "manifestations" had taken place. A candle having been lighted, the brothers were seen still bound to their chairs, while some of the instruments had dropped into the laps of the visitors. I myself received a blow on the face from a floating guitar.

The evening concluded with a startling demonstration. William Fay was bound to a chair. His hands were tied behind his back. The lights were extinguished; and a whizzing sound was heard.

"It's off," he announced.

The lights came back on. Fay was still tied to the chair. *But his coat had been removed.* It was lying on the floor. And the spirits were not yet finished, reports the *Post*:

> Astonishing though this appeared to be, what followed was more extraordinary still. Dr. Ferguson requested a gentle-

> man present to take off his coat and place it on the table. This was done, the light was extinguished, a repetition of the whizzing noise was heard, and the strange coat was found upon Mr. Fay, whose hands and feet were still securely bound, and his body tied almost immovably to the chair.

The audience ("which included some of the sharpest minds in England," says Nichols) was amazed. How could this feat be explained? How could a medium, restrained by ropes, shed his coat and then don another? Had he indeed been aided by spirits?

Conceivably so, according to one reporter. "We had witnessed an annihilation of what we call 'material laws,' or were we the dupes of extremely clever conjuring?...I must confess that the verdict of 'conjuring' was not that which was pronounced by my companions."

Another speculated that "some new physical force" had been involved. The manifestations had taken place, he insisted, "under conditions and circumstances that preclude the presumption of fraud....All that can be said is, that the manifestations of Messrs. Davenport and Mr. Fay appear to be altogether inexplicable."

Yet for others, fraud was not to be precluded as an explanation. In fact, it *was* the explanation. The brothers were nothing more than escape artists, able to untie themselves and produce the manifestations. And as the private séances continued, in a succession of drawing-rooms, the press became increasingly vocal in its skepticism:

> "From beginning to end, a piece of flagrant jugglery" (*Standard*)
>
> "Grotesquely absurd" (*Saturday Review*)
>
> "A common case of conjuring, managed by a secret entrance into the apartment behind the cabinet" (*Spectator*)
>
> "It is both surprising and deplorable that persons of education and standing should not only countenance but welcome and applaud such efforts, and that influential organs

> of opinion should be found ready to give them indirect encouragement, if not positive support." (*Daily News*)
>
> "We trust that public curiosity will not encourage the sham. It means, if anything, that spirits—powers hovering between earth and heaven—help a man off with his coat, tinkle a muffin-bell, play upon banjoes, touch people's knees, rap them on the knuckles, and play a hundred fantastic tricks, which cease immediately upon the lighting of a farthing candle. It is too much!" (*Herald*)

But the brothers welcomed the publicity that was brought on by controversy. They began to hold public séances, which were well-attended. Many in the audience were Spiritualists. W. S. Gilbert (the librettist half of Gilbert and Sullivan), in his weekly column for *Fun,* described these believers:

> They were all gaunt and angular, with very large bony noses and hollow cheeks. They conversed in mysterious whispers....a certain section of spiritualists attend every seance held by the Davenport brothers, from motives analogous to those which induce the still un-humbugged portion of society to go once a week to church. The sceptics dropped in later, and as your own correspondent discovered among these latter several cheerful friends who were disposed to take a lively view of the proceedings in general, he passed an exceedingly pleasant evening.*

Were the Davenports fraudulent, as their detractors maintained? And if so, how might they be exposed? A practical suggestion was offered by the *Globe.* The newspaper urged that the brothers be tested—by conjurers, not scientists. For who was better suited to detect trickery than its foremost practitioners? And three London magicians—Anderson, Tolmaque, and Redmond—did seek to expose them. Professor Anderson, then appearing at St. James's

---

* *Fun* was a satirical publication that competed with *Punch. Punch* too found the Davenports to be a source of amusement, calling them "Ministers of the Interior, with a seat in the Cabinet."

Hall, gave "an exhibition after the manner of the Brothers Davenport." He demonstrated that their miracles could be reproduced by "natural agency"—that is to say, by employing the techniques of a conjurer.

Yet despite the charges of fraud, many were convinced that the brothers were genuine mediums. In a letter to the *Newcastle Chronicle,* one supporter wrote:

> I have seen nearly all the greatest conjurors of the present day. I have been behind the scenes, and assisted in making the necessary preparations for a wizard's entertainment. I have seen both M. Tolmaque and Mr. Redmond do their rope-trick, and I know how it is done. I can honestly declare that what the Davenports do as far surpasses Anderson, Tolmaque, and Redmond, as these gentlemen can surpass such a clumsy amateur as I am. I am totally at a loss to account for the Davenports' feats by any known principle of legerdemain. If what they do is conjuring, all I can say about it is, that it is the cleverest conjuring I ever saw or heard of.

And their strongest supporter was still Dion Boucicault, who encouraged scientists to study the manifestations. Lovers of truth, says Nichols, were indebted to Boucicault, "for an exhibition of so much candour, moral courage, and genuine philosophy, which I cannot but think more in character for English gentlemen than the sneers, ridicule, and flagrant abuse of a portion of the press of this metropolis." The actor hosted a second séance in his drawing-room, to which he invited more of his distinguished friends. Among those who gathered that night were Viscount Bury, Sir Charles Nicholson (Ambassador to Mexico), Captain Inglefield (the Arctic navigator), two physicians, several journalists, and the Chancellor of the University of Sydney. All were eager to witness the phenomena.

The brothers had come a long way since that first manifestation in Buffalo, when the family had laid their hands on a table in a darkened parlor...and the table had shook.

"Marriage"

Adah Menken had arrived in London in May of 1864; the Davenport brothers, in September. By the end of the year, both the actress and the mediums had become celebrities. *Mazeppa* was playing to full houses; and Menken's suite at the Palace Hotel had become a gathering place for the artistic elite—a salon. Meanwhile, the Davenport séances were drawing large audiences; and like *Mazeppa,* had created a stir. "The chief excitements at this moment," reported the London correspondent for the *New York Times,* "are Miss Menken bound to her fiery steed...and the brothers Davenport bound to their chairs."

And the paths of these celebrities crossed, thanks to a mutual acquaintance. Dion Boucicault (who, like Murdock, had an eye for the ladies) had befriended Adah Menken. One night he escorted her to the Davenport séance; and afterwards, took her backstage to meet the brothers. Intrigued by their aura of mystery, she invited them to the next gathering in her hotel suite.

No less intrigued by *her* aura, the brothers showed up. Menken introduced them to the other guests and chatted with them about Spiritualism. The Davenports talked about their life as itinerant mediums—the traveling from town to town; the posting of posters; the exhibiting in local halls. And Menken realized that these "mystics" were in fact entertainers—stalwart troupers like herself. She also found herself attracted to William.

Why William and not Ira? The brothers closely resembled one other—so much so that they were often taken for twins. Both were handsome, well-spoken, and intelligent. Yet their personalities were strikingly different. In *The Davenport Brothers,* Randolph contrasts the two:

> But socially there is a marked difference; for whereas Ira is full of life and vivacity, William is remarkable for the sober gentleness of his demeanor; the one is the incarnation of good feeling, life, and gladness, and the other of delicate

> sensitiveness, rapidity of perception, intuition, and calm dignity.

In other words, Ira was outgoing and sociable, while William had more of an artistic temperament. So when Adah Menken—actress, poet, and bohemian—wound up having an affair with one of the Davenports, it was with William, the younger brother.

They conducted their affair in secret. For Menken was still married (to a husband—her third—whom she had left behind in New York); and not even "the naked lady" dared to challenge the Victorian era's condemnation of adultery. But she did declare the brothers to be her "spiritual advisors." And she attended their séances with a horsewhip, threatening to punish anyone who tied them too tightly.

The affair was also conducted intermittently. For after their triumphs in London, both Menken and the Davenports went on tour; and months would pass without the actress and the medium seeing one another. Yet despite these separations, they remained passionately involved.

So much so that they regarded themselves as married. Early in January of 1865, they had registered incognito at a small hotel outside of London. And Menken had sat down and penned an oath:

> I...acknowledge Wm. H. Davenport, as my only legal and beloved husband for all my future life, so help me God I believe to be my Father and of all earth. Signed by me, A. I. Menken.

She had then signed the oath with the initials "A. I. M. D."

This "marriage" was in no way legal (especially since Menken already had a husband). It did serve though to strengthen the tie between them.*

Rude Receptions

After months in London, conducting séances in private homes and a public hall, the Davenports embarked upon a tour of the provinces. Initially, the tour was a success, with their exhibition well-received in Yorkshire and Lancashire. But in Liverpool came a change of fortune.

A private séance in Liverpool had been favorably

---

* Their relationship would remain a secret (or at least an unsubstantiated rumor) until 1993, when Ormus Davenport, the great-grandson of Ira, published an article titled "The Davenport Brothers and Adah Isaacs Menken." The brothers' scrapbook, diaries, letters, and other memorabilia had been passed down in the family; and Ormus had become their caretaker. He used them as the basis for the article, which appeared in *The Linking Ring,* a journal for magicians. Ormus's son inherited this treasure-trove, and donated the scrapbook to Lily Dale, the Spiritualist village. It is filled with newspaper clippings—the earliest from 1856—that document the career of the Davenport brothers. As for the diaries and letters, I have been unable to learn their present location.

The scrapbook is described in "Magicians Among the Spirits" in *Real-Life X-Files: Investigating the Paranormal* (2001) by Joe Nickell, who spotted it on display in the museum at Lily Dale.

reviewed (the manifestations were described as "most strange and entirely unaccountable"). And a public séance, held in St. George's Hall, drew a large crowd. The evening began in the usual way. Ferguson delivered his lecture and introduced the Davenports. Then he called for volunteers to bind them. And up leapt two rough-looking fellows named Hulley and Cummins—"a couple of evil spirits," reported the *Telegraph,* who would prove "more than a match for the good angels who hover about the Davenports."

The two were given ropes and told to bind the brothers securely. They began to do so—in a brutal fashion, as tightly as possible. The pain was intolerable; and the brothers insisted that they stop and let someone else perform the binding. But Hulley and Cummins refused to step aside and were cheered by the audience. At an impasse, the Davenports refused to continue. The séance was postponed until the following night, with a refund given to anyone requesting it.

But Hulley and Cummins were determined to humiliate the Davenports, whom they deemed to be humbugs. And what happened that second night is described by the brothers themselves, in a statement they issued:

> On the following evening, printed regulations were given to every person entering the hall, and read from the platform; in which we distinctly claimed the right of rejecting any person on a committee whom we should find acting with unfairness. This would be our right were we criminals on trial for felony. Before commencing, we invited all persons who were not satisfied with these regulations to retire from the hall, and receive the money they had paid for entrance.
>
> Messrs. Hulley and Cummins, backed by a crowd of their friends, came again upon the platform, and, from their previous unfairness, were promptly rejected by us as a committee. They insisted upon tying us, and appealed to the audience to support them in their demand. They refused to leave the platform when requested, took possession of our cabinet, and in various ways excited violent manifestations in the audience.

> We were then assured by a gentleman of Liverpool, that, unless we submitted to the demands of these men, there would be a furious riot. He promised that they should not be permitted to injure us, and we finally yielded to his assurances. But they had no sooner placed the cords upon our wrists, than they inflicted a degree of pain which could not be endured. We protested against this violence, but in vain; and, refusing to submit to it longer, had the cords cut from our wrists, and left the platform, which was instantly invaded by the mob. Our cabinet was broken in pieces; and Hulley and Cummins, the heroes of this assault of some hundreds of brave Englishmen upon four unarmed, unoffending, and unprotected foreigners, were borne from the hall upon the shoulders of their friends, apparently proud of their triumph.

Amazingly, Ira and William were undaunted:

> Our cabinet destroyed, and our business interrupted, with heavy pecuniary damage, in Liverpool, we returned to London, had a new cabinet constructed, and on the following Monday repaired to Halifax, where we gave our usual public and private exhibitions, without interruption.

But Halifax would prove to be the exception. At each subsequent stop on the tour, trouble awaited them. In Huddersfield, only the presence of the police prevented another riot, the violence "expending itself in hooting and howling." In Hull, the proprietor of the hall cancelled their engagement, fearing damage to his property. And in Leeds, a mob once again stormed the stage. The cabinet was destroyed; the musical instruments were stolen; the brothers were mocked. "It may be doubted," they lamented, "if such an amount of violence, wrong, and outrage has been inflicted on any unoffending man in England since Clarkson was mobbed by the slave-traders of Liverpool, and Priestley by the mad bigots of Birmingham."

This time the Davenports were discouraged. Their welcome in England had apparently expired. It was time, they decided, to move on.

Paris

With nearly a thousand seats, the Salle Herz was the largest hall in Paris. And on the night of September 14, 1865, it was sold-out, for the first public séance of the Davenports. But the brothers noted something suspicious: a hundred of the less expensive tickets, for seats in the rear, had been sold to one party. And they knew who that probably was: Henri Robin, the magician who had become their outspoken opponent.

The brothers had arrived in Paris several months earlier. And they had conducted private séances at a chateau outside the city, while awaiting a permit to give public performances. Attended by journalists, these séances had succeeded in generating publicity. But they had also provoked Robin, who issued statements accusing the Davenports of fakery. And at his Théâtre Robin he gave exhibitions that duplicated their "spirit manifestations," and that demonstrated how they were able to untie themselves. Apparently, he was now planning to disrupt the séance at the Herz, with a pack of hired ruffians.

The evening began with a speech by the interpreter. He presented the Davenports and offered their usual disclaimer. They introduce themselves to you, he told the audience in French, neither as wizards nor as conjurers; they propose simply to enable you to witness phenomena, of the causes of which they themselves are ignorant, leaving you alone to judge the effects which will be produced.

Two volunteers were selected: a cousin of the Emperor and a newspaper editor. Both were well-known and respected, and could not be accused of collusion. They examined the cabinet, looking for secret springs or other contrivances. None were found. Then they bound the brothers—so securely that escape was impossible, they assured the audience—and shut the cabinet doors.

When the doors were reopened just minutes later, the Davenports were revealed to be unbound. The spirits had untied them! Suddenly a spectator leapt onto the stage. He denounced the brothers as tricksters; claimed the seats contained hidden springs; and with a vigorous blow, broke one of the seats.

Others in the audience came onto the stage, wanting to see for themselves. "The performance was lost in a tumult worthy of a meeting of infuriated shareholders," the editor would report. "After about three-quarters of an hour's row, the spectators had to be cleared out of the hall with the police at their back."

A more detailed account is found in *The Brothers Davenport*; and it makes clear who was responsible for the tumult. According to Randolph, one of Robin's hirelings stood up in the rear and demanded permission to examine the cabinet. The interpreter denied the request. It was contrary to the rules, he explained, for anyone other than the volunteers—who represented the audience—to come onto the stage.

> This announcement was received with applause by the majority of the audience; but it was soon evident, from the vociferous noises and loud demands that he be permitted to go upon the stage from parties in the rear of the hall, that there was an organized conspiracy to interrupt the *séance.* Great confusion ensued; and several American gentlemen, visitors in Paris, who sat near the stage, said to the brothers, that, if it was their wish not to comply with this demand, they would protect them in resisting it, at the hazard of their lives. The brothers consulted; and as such disturbance might be considered sufficient pretext by the police for closing the *séance* altogether, as they have power to do, it was decided to allow this man to come upon the stage. The manifestations were resumed, the doors of the cabinet were opened, and the brothers found secure, when suddenly this man rushed to the cabinet, and placing his back against one side, and his feet against the upright post in the centre, he wrenched away by main force the cross-bar into which the seats are fastened; the boys, thus bound, falling forward with the seats. Triumphantly holding up this broken stick to the audience, he declared that he had discovered secret springs.

In fact, the "springs" were simply hinges that facilitated the dismantling of the cabinet for transport. But the accusation prompted an uproar in the hall. Fearing a riot, the chief of police mounted the stage and ordered everyone to leave. His men cleared the hall; and ticket-money was refunded. Many refused the refund, expressing satisfaction with the manifestations they had witnessed. Others were detected demanding a refund twice. The séance had ended prematurely and unprofitably, thanks to the enmity of Robin.

In the days that followed, the Davenports were allowed to conduct séances in a smaller hall at the Herz. But audiences were limited by the police to sixty persons—a financial calamity. And then, on a Saturday afternoon, they received an unexpected notice. Emperor Napoleon III had summoned the brothers to appear—that very night—at the palace of St. Cloud. A command performance! They hastened to arrange for the transport of the cabinet.

> They arrived at St. Cloud about nine o'clock, and found some thirty distinguished persons of the court assembled, and among them the Emperor and Empress, also the young Prince Imperial, a fine, active little fellow, who was anxious to have them teach him the trick, as he called it.
>
> During the process of erecting the cabinet, which occupied about three-quarters of an hour, his Majesty was present, and looked on with the greatest interest, closely scrutinizing every part as it was properly adjusted. Everything being in readiness, the company being seated, two persons came forward, and, in a very scientific and skilful manner, commenced binding the brothers, his Majesty standing near, and examining every cord and knot placed upon them. The Empress, upon one occasion, thinking the ropes upon their wrists were too tightly drawn, ordered them to be slackened, and would only allow the tying to proceed after the most positive assurance on their part that the cords caused them no inconvenience.

The lights were lowered; the doors were shut; and the manifestations began. The trumpet flew out of the aperture, landing not far from the Emperor. The musical instruments sounded; the ghostly hands flashed. Then one of the courtiers joined the brothers inside the cabinet. Upon emerging, he reported that he had rested a hand on each of them in the dark, and that the brothers had remained motionless—yet singular events had taken place. And the séance concluded with the mysterious removal of Fay's coat—a feat that elicited, says Randolph, "an exclamation of wonder and surprise from the company."

Afterwards, the Emperor and Empress chatted with the Davenports. They asked questions about the causes of the phenomena, and expressed their satisfaction with the exhibition. Finally, at half-past one in the morning, the imperial party withdrew. And Ira and William sat down to a sumptuous supper that was provided for them in the palace.

The next day they received "an unusually munificent gift for their services." The losses suffered at the Herz were more than compensated.

As for Robin, he would suffer a blow to his career. Robert Cooper, author of *Spiritual Experiences, Including Seven Months with the Brothers Davenport* (1867), tells of it:

> A few days after, Robin gave his exhibition—a professed exposure of the Davenports—at the palace. It was supposed at the time, by those who knew the Emperor to be a believer in spiritual phenomena, that his object in sending for Robin was from motives of policy, but it subsequently transpired that it was done to allay the excitement of the youthful Prince, who witnessed the Davenport exhibition and had since done nothing but talk about the "spirits." The Emperor pronounced Robin's performance the greatest rubbish he had ever seen.

End of a "Marriage"

A year after that oath, Adah Menken and William Davenport quarreled and separated. The actress had learned that she was pregnant. William's reaction to the news was likely the cause of their quarrel.

In a letter to Eliza Fay, Menken described herself as "lonely, bereaved and neglected by the only being I actually love." And a few days later, from the Swan Hotel in Bolton, she wrote to William:

> Darling Will,
>
> Your last brief letter came to Cheltenham.... Do not sympathize for yourself, but for me—I suffer. I love you. I must act here tomorrow night. My heart pains me. I long to see you. You say you are going to America without a regret of leaving me. I dare say you are right. I am not worthy to be thought of. But I love you. You are good and I can never forget. Forgive me if I have ever wronged in word or thought—I have only been jealous through love, and you did not deserve it. Oh, think kindly of me as you can. I feel, dear William, how I have lost your love, but no tears so bitter than mine, no repentance so severe. Pray for me. Ask God to remember me. I suffer. I love you. I am ill and despairing. Write if you can. Your poor wife. A. I. M. D.

But they remained estranged. And the child was born eight months later, in Paris.

Almost immediately, Menken returned to the stage, starring in *Les Pirates de la Savane* at the Théâtre de la Gaité. Opening night was sold-out. An expectant audience awaited their first glimpse of the celebrity actress. Seated among them was William, who had yielded to her entreaties and come to see her.

She took nine curtain calls that night, to thunderous applause. And later, in her dressing room, she waited for William to appear. But a crowd of admirers had gathered outside the stage door; and he was unable to make his way through.

The crowd was still there when she emerged from the theatre. William called out her name; and she saw him. "Your hotel in an hour!" he shouted.

There, amid tears and promises of fidelity, the two reconciled. But they were soon to be parted. For the Davenports were about to embark upon a tour of European cities that would take them as far as St. Petersburg.

La belle Menken became a sensation in Paris. Once again she hosted a salon and socialized with the artistic elite. As a poet, Menken was especially drawn to writers; and she became friendly with Alexander Dumas *père*. A studio photograph of them was widely circulated. It showed Menken perched beside the novelist, smiling fondly and resting her head on his shoulder. The photograph prompted rumors of an affair. Whether true or not, the rumors pleased the aging, corpulent Dumas; and he did not deny them.

Upon his return to Paris, William saw the photograph; fell into a jealous rage; and ended his "marriage" with Menken.

Australia

In August 1868, at the age of 33, Menken died in her hotel room in Paris. The exact cause of her death was unknown; but for weeks she had been ill and unable to rehearse. William was in London at the time. When he heard the news, he drank himself into a stupor.

After four years abroad, the Davenports were about to return to America. Those years had brought them fame and fortune; but it was time to go home. And in September they sailed from Glasgow to New York.

During the next six years they traveled about as before, transporting the cabinet from town to town and conducting séances. There were two new members of the troupe. One was Louise, an attractive Belgian woman who had caught Ira's eye during one of the séances in Paris. After a brief courtship—facilitated by an interpreter, as neither spoke the other's language—they had wed. It was Ira's second marriage. In 1862, while touring in Michigan, he had married a local woman. But the marriage had been brief: she had died in childbirth. The other addition was young Harry Kellar, hired as an assistant. Kellar would become the foremost magician in America.

In 1875 the Davenports traveled to Australia, for a series

of engagements. They were perhaps seeking a fresh start, in a distant land, after incidents such as this:

> THE DAVENPORT BROTHERS CAUGHT.—The Davenport Brothers lately gave some of their psychic exhibitions at Ithaca, New York, but their tricks were sadly disarranged by some of the Cornell University fellows. A private letter says that some of the students, having a scientific turn of mind, provided themselves beforehand with pyrotechnic balls containing phosphorus, so made as to ignite suddenly with a bright light. During the dark seances, when the Davenports purported to be, and as the audience supposed were, bound hand and foot...and when the guitar was floating in the air and playing musically around, the aforesaid students struck their lights all of a sudden, when the spirits were found to be none other than the Davenports themselves, who were dodging about the stage, brandishing the guitars, and playing the tunes. The music suddenly ceased, the committee declared the performance a humbug, and the players departed from Ithaca by the earliest train. (Baltimore *Sun*, February 1, 1872)

Their stay in Australia lasted for two years and was a financial success. But the basic premise of the exhibitions had changed. No longer were the mysterious goings-on—the manifestations inside the cabinet, the removal of Fay's jacket—attributed to spirits. Instead, the Davenports and "Professor Fay" presented themselves as escape artists. They challenged volunteers to bind them so securely as to make it impossible to get free. And other entertainers were included now in the show. Traveling with the brothers were E. D. Davies, billed as the "Premier Ventriloquist of the World," and his daughter Eva, who played the piano. Moreover, there was a new emphasis on comedy. A local official, clergyman, or other prominent person would be selected to join the brothers inside the cabinet. Upon emerging, he had the tambourine on his head; his tie had been removed; and the ropes were draped around him. A dignitary had been made to look like a fool; and the audience responded with gleeful laughter. The séance had been transformed into an escape act and comedy routine. No longer needed were the spirits.

There was no shortage of bookings for the Davenports. But William had grown increasingly ill, with a lung ailment. And in July 1877—three months after marrying Eva—he died in a Sydney hotel. The brothers had been unusually close. For twenty years they had performed as a duo. They had shared the rigors of the road, the confined space of the cabinet, and the vagaries of fortune; and Ira was devastated by the loss.

Mayville

Ira retired to the town of Mayville, on the northern shore of Lake Chautauqua. And except for that failed attempt, fifteen years later, to revive the act, he no longer climbed into the cabinet. With him in Mayville were Louise and their three children. After years of residing in hotels, they had settled at last into a home of their own.

He entertained the children with stories of the Davenport brothers—their misadventures, travels, and triumphs. Over the years, the memories of those events had mellowed into nostalgia. And fading now from public consciousness were memories of the brothers themselves.

Then, in 1909, Ira—now seventy years old—received a letter from Houdini. A fan letter! While on tour, Houdini had run into Harry Kellar. And he had been surprised to learn, not only that his fellow magician had once worked for the Davenports, but that Ira was still living. Houdini immediately wrote to him; and a correspondence ensued. For in the Davenport brothers, Houdini had recognized his predecessors. They were the original escapologists—"pioneers," he called them, "in the mystic art of rope-tying."

The following year Houdini was in Australia, for a three-month engagement in theatres there. During his stay he tracked down the grave of William Davenport. "Finding it sadly neglected," he reports in *A Magician Among the Spirits* (1924), "I had it put in order, fresh flowers planted on it and the stone work repaired." He had a photograph taken of himself at the restored gravesite—a photograph that he would present to a grateful Ira.

Also, he met with Fay, who had settled in Australia and become wealthy from real-estate investments. Fay reminisced about his years with the Davenports—years the adventure of which he missed. "He is not at all contented," Ira had written to Houdini, "notwithstanding his pleasant surroundings and ample fortune; after a man has become a regular 'Globe Trotter,' I don't think it possible for him to settle down and lead a quiet monotonous life."

Yet Ira himself had found contentment in such a life, as Houdini would discover. One of the first things Houdini did upon returning to the U.S. was to take a train to Mayville and visit his correspondent. Ira welcomed him and introduced him to Louise and their daughter Zellie. Houdini describes their home as "an exceptionally happy and restful one," and Ira and Louise as "a remarkably happy couple."

The house had a porch that overlooked Lake Chautauqua. It was a breezy day in July. The two men settled into chairs on the porch and talked. "We turned back the pages of time, Mr. Davenport re-living in retrospect the trials, battles, praise and applause of long ago." Ira described the spirit cabinet and the séances that had featured it. He assured Houdini that nothing supernatural had been involved; the manifestations had been effected by natural means—through physical dexterity. He and his brother had been escape artists, he confessed, and nothing more. He regaled Houdini with stories of their early days, and of their later career—the success at the Cooper Institute; the disaster in Liverpool; the performance for the Tsar in St. Petersburg. And as Houdini took notes, Ira revealed the secret of their feats:

> For me it was a memorable day and did not end with the setting of the sun, for we talked far into the night, I with notebook in hand, he with a long piece of rope initiating

> me into the mysteries of the real "Davenport tie," which converted thousands to a belief in Spiritualism.... Though many attempts were made to imitate it, to the best of my knowledge and belief, no one, not even the magical fraternity, was ever able to detect the method used in these famous rope tricks, the secret being guarded so carefully that Ira Davenport's children did not know it.

First of all, said Ira, they would induce the volunteer to tie them in such a way as would facilitate their escape. And as their wrists were being tied, the brothers were able to secure a few inches of slack in the rope. This slack was the secret of the Davenport Tie. Taken up, it made the rope less taut. And this loosening, along with Vaseline, dexterity, and determination, enabled them to work their hands free—to slide their hands out of the loops. They were then able to play on the musical instruments or to further extricate themselves.

And because the manifestations could be produced, if necessary, by a single person, being a duo served the brothers as insurance. On those rare occasions where one of them was unable to free his hands, the other, in all probability, would succeed. "There was only one chance in twenty million to hold us both at the same time."

Finally, the Davenports had used only a particular type of rope: Silver Lake sash cord. Intended for windows, it was both stiff and smooth—qualities that made it ideal for an escape artist.*

That night on the porch Ira had revealed their secrets; and Houdini had taken notes. The moon hung over Lake Chautauqua, like a spotlight on the two of them. "Houdini, we started it, you finish it," said Ira. The torch had been passed.

---

* "With this style of rope, it is an almost utter impossibility to be tied but what you can free yourself," says William Robinson in *Spirit Slate Writing and Kindred Phenomena* (1898). (Robinson was the magician who performed as Chung Ling Soo.) "Very few persons can tie a medium securely with the stiff rope furnished."

And there had been witnesses to its passing:

> Long after Ira died his only daughter, Zellie, a well known actress, told me that while her father and I were so absorbed in discussing and experimenting with the rope trick she and her mother cautiously slipped behind the curtains and watched us through the bed-room window.

The Real Mystery

The Davenports were conjurers who presented themselves (albeit with a disclaimer) as mediums—as intermediaries between this world and the next. And many were persuaded that their powers were genuine. According to Houdini, their mysteries had "converted thousands to a belief in Spiritualism." Yet those mysteries were illusions—the skilled work of a pair of escape artists.

What was their attitude, one wonders, to the deception they practiced, with its assurances of an afterlife? Especially problematic was the position of Ira, who seems to have been a Spiritualist himself. Among the clippings in their scrapbook is an obituary for his first wife, who had died in childbirth. Probably written by Ira himself, its heading is "Passed to Spirit Life." And it says of her:

> Possessing a highly refined and cultivated mind and fully realizing the importance of the great truths of spiritualism, she exercised an elevated influence over her husband in properly directing his energies and mediumistic powers, for the advancement of the facts of immortality.

Pasted in with the obituary are pious poems, clipped from newspapers.

And on his own tombstone in Mayville is carved a rising sun, and the epitaph THERE NEVER WAS NIGHT THAT HAD NO MORN.

How Ira reconciled a belief in Spiritualism with his career as a pseudo-medium is the real mystery of the Davenport brothers.

Professor Solomon's
LIVES OF THE CONJURERS
VOLUME ONE
SIGNOR BLITZ
BOX BROWN
CAGLIOSTRO
HOCUS POCUS
BOTTLE CONJURER
HELLER
TORRINI
FAWKES
ROBERTSON
BANGS SISTERS
BERT REESE
MORRITT
C.W. STARR
HENRY SLADE
LE ROY & TALMA
MAURER
KATTERFELTO
MAELZEL
Biographies of the great magicians!

www.ingramcontent.com/pod-product-compliance
Lightning Source LLC
Chambersburg PA
CBHW060505030426
42337CB00015B/1744

* 9 7 8 0 9 1 2 5 0 9 1 6 7 *